'BORDER BREEZE'

A TRUE STORY BY

DEBBIE SAXTON

Published by New Generation Publishing in 2022

Copyright © Debbie Saxton 2022

First Edition

The author asserts the moral right under the Copyright, Designs and Patents Act 1988 to be identified as the author of this work.

All Rights reserved. No part of this publication may be reproduced, stored in a retrieval system or transmitted, in any form or by any means without the prior consent of the author, nor be otherwise circulated in any form of binding or cover other than that which it is published and without a similar condition being imposed on the subsequent purchaser.

ISBN   978-1-80369-288-3

www.newgeneration-publishing.com

New Generation Publishing

DEDICATION

I would like to dedicate this book firstly to my late grandfather Albert Backhouse, from whom I inherited my love for horses. He took me to my first riding lesson when I was five years old. Sadly, our journey together was cut short following his sudden untimely death only two years later. I continued what should have been our journey, in his memory.

Secondly, Julie and Bill for all their continued support over the years.

Finally, my long-suffering husband John. He has been on this long road with me, enduring many ups and many more downs. I would have lost my sanity at times without him by my side supporting all the decisions I have made.

Chapter 1

I remember the fun my friends and I used to have when we were young. There was no greater thrill than galloping through the open fields bareback with the wind in our hair, just holding on to the top of the horse's headcollar, which we also used to steer. No reins. We were absolutely fearless.

We would spend endless summer days hacking around the beautiful surrounding countryside where we were lucky enough to live. They were great days, which I remember with lots of fond memories as if they had happened only yesterday.

Leaving school and starting work led me to other interests though, mainly going out most nights with friends and my interest in horses faded slightly. Sadly, I made the decision to sell my pony. I always thought one day I would buy another one and pick up my childhood passion again but I never thought it would take me twenty-five years!

....

I had not even sat on a horse in twenty-five years, let alone ridden one. I was now married with two sons of school age. We were due to move shortly to a beautiful house complete with access to land and stables, so I decided this was the perfect opportunity to start riding again and hopefully one day soon, own another horse.

Coinciding with this, I had stayed in touch with one of my oldest friends from my riding days. Although we hadn't seen each other much over the years, we had always continued to exchange cards at Christmas and write updates in them of what we had been doing over the past twelve months. It was after the 2004 card that my life changed dramatically. Julie wrote her phone number in the card and asked if I'd like to meet up? I instantly called her and within a week, we were sat in a local pub catching up over a drink. It was wonderful to see her again, we had so much to talk about. Conversation soon came around to the passion and love of horses that we both shared.

Julie told me all about her three horses which she had bred herself. During the conversation, I told her about my hopes of buying another horse at some point. She suggested I go and have a few riding lessons to get me back in the saddle, then go over to her farm and ride one of her horses. I loved this idea. So much so, I rang the local riding school first thing the following morning and booked my first lesson! I couldn't wait to start riding again and was so excited at the prospect of riding with Julie after all these years. That evening I phoned her to let her know and arranged to go to her farm to meet her horses that coming weekend.

Obviously, it had been a long time since I'd sat on a horse so it seemed sensible to book myself some riding lessons. I wanted to be sure this was a hobby I did want to pursue again before I went to the expense of buying a horse and committing to all the endless hours I knew would be involved in its keep.

I found my old riding hat in the loft but it was too small! No surprises there though, my grandfather bought it for me when I was five years old! So, I went off to shop for a new hat. Also, on this trip I would pick up some jodhpurs and a pair of long riding boots. I could not believe the choice! It was vast compared to twenty-five years ago.

Whilst I was there I perused the horse section to make a mental list of what I would need for my next horse. The rug section was baffling. Where was the 'New Zealand Rug'? That's what everyone had back in the day. Now there seemed to be light weights, medium weights and heavy weights coming in all different thicknesses, fly rugs, coolers, fleeces; the lists, colours and designs were endless.

With a hat, jodhpurs and riding boots in my basket, I headed to the till to pay. I picked up a headcollar and lead rope intending to buy them alongside my other purchases.

'What are you buying those for?' asked my husband.

'My new horse,' I replied.

'You haven't got a horse, put them back, it's a waste of money,' he said. I did as he asked, which was rare. Julie and I still laugh about this now. I actually put them back to save a few pounds. Within a year, I'd spent thousands!

The day of my first lesson arrived. I finished work at 2 pm and drove to the riding school. I had my hat, jodhpurs, boots and a jacket in the car and managed to change into them in the car in the car park.

I was suddenly really nervous and excited at the same time as I walked across the yard into the office. There was a lady behind the reception desk. I gave her my name and announced I had a lesson booked.

'Follow me,' she said.

We went out of the office and across the yard to an American-style stable block. Inside there were probably around twenty horses, all stood in their individual stalls eating hay. In the first stall was a beautiful black mare. She had her bridle and saddle on and would be the horse I would be having my lesson on.

My instructor came forward, introduced herself, untied the horse and led her out of the stall by the reins. She asked about my riding ability, so I explained. I hadn't been a novice rider all those years ago, but equally many years had passed so I was unsure what level I would be now. I felt like I was starting from scratch again.

She led the horse to a mounting block. I took the reins in my left hand and put my left foot in the stirrup. I swung my right leg over and put my foot in the other stirrup. The horse was around 15.2 hands and with me being 5 foot 4 inches, it was a good size for me, although too big for me to mount from the ground as I seemed to have zero flexibility. I have to say, once back on board, it felt like I had never had a break. It was amazing to actually be sat on a horse again after all these years. I took to it again like a duck to water. I had a lovely instructor who took me to the indoor school and put me through my paces. The thirty-minute lesson was exhausting – it made me realise as a self-taught rider, I definitely had picked up plenty of bad habits as a child. My instructor was constantly telling me to sit up straight, push my legs back, keep my heels down and hands level. I found it hard to do all these things at the same time but felt a sense of satisfaction when they all came together. I walked, trotted and even had a little canter by the end of the lesson. I went home with a huge smile on my face.

I returned to the stables several times over the following weeks and gained more confidence in the school. By now I was pretty confident walking, trotting and cantering and was managing to keep a good position and loved being back in the saddle again.

Although it was great being in the school, I did find it limiting. I was never one for riding round and round in a manège. In fact, I found it incredibly boring. I wanted to hack out in the beautiful countryside I was so lucky to be surrounded by.

I arranged for my next visit to the riding school to be for an hour-long hack-out. It was February and the weather was as you would expect for the time of year. On this particular day, it was horrendous. I was in two minds whether to cancel my ride, but if you decided to only ride on warm sunny days in England, there would probably not be many opportunities. The sky was black and the wind was howling. When I arrived at the stables, two horses were tacked up and ready to go and I thought, *There's no turning back now*. We led the horses out into the yard and in turn my instructor and I mounted using the mounting block. Girths adjusted, we proceeded out of the yard and onto the road. So far so good. We trotted along the road and turned left, heading off up a steep country lane. At this point the sleet started. It was blowing into my face and I could not see where I was going. I rode tucked behind my instructor but I could not hear what she was saying.

As we turned onto a grassy track, the sleet had turned to snow and it was coming down fast and furious. As soon as we hit the track, that was it; my horse went off like a bat out of hell at full-speed gallop. I could not see for the snow; the ground was uneven and my horse was stumbling all over the place. I felt totally out of control, I was pulling hard on the reins and found myself standing up in my stirrups pulling with all my might, but it made no difference, the horse was following the one in front and there was nothing I could do to slow her down. I just grabbed a handful of mane and made it my mission to try and stay on. The track soon came to an end and we stopped briefly whilst I composed myself before we headed back down the lane to the stables to get out of the harsh weather. It was a relief to finally dismount and be heading home to get out of my soaked clothes.

I did note that day that riding-school horses are set in their routine and they are literally on auto-pilot. They follow the horse in front at the pace the horse in front goes! Once back home that day, feeling a great sense of achievement, I decided the time was right for me to move up to the next level.

I went over to Julie's stables the following weekend to hack out with her. I had already met her horses by now so knew I would be riding Belle, a beautiful chestnut half-Arabian/half-Section D mare. I was keen to try long-distance endurance riding, and with Belle standing at 14.1 hands she was an ideal size for me to mount without the need of a mounting block. This discipline can bring many challenges, especially when you are riding for miles into the unknown. You need to be sure if you have to dismount for any reason, for example, to open an awkward gate, you need to be able to mount again quickly without assistance and get on your way. There may not always be a handy wall to stand on to use as a mounting block!

In many ways I was spoilt by Belle, she was such a dream to ride and I became obsessed with looking to own my own horse again. By this point, my mind was made up – it was time to start looking for my perfect horse. I knew exactly what I wanted. It was not difficult for me to paint a picture of what my ideal horse would be. My last pony, twenty-five years earlier, had been a 13.2 grey Connemara. Had I bought another horse straight after her, without question it would have been an Arabian. My vision was a bay mare, part or full Arabian, 14.2 hands maximum. Must be bombproof in traffic, good to travel and good for a farrier to shoe.

Chapter 2

I began searching advertisements on websites and in magazines for my perfect horse. It was not as easy as I thought it was going to be. It would be several weeks before I would spot the first advert which would be of any interest to me. A bay mare fitting the description I was looking for, and she looked stunning on the photographs.

She was a dark bay, part-bred Arab and although she stood at 14.2 hands, she was of a fine build possibly too fine, but I made arrangements to see her. Julie would be coming with me as I thought it would be much better if I had a valued second opinion.

My husband drove and we picked Julie up on the way. We arrived to see this beautiful dark bay mare. I just felt that she sadly wouldn't be the one for me. She looked smaller than 14.2 hands and didn't feel solid enough to carry me. Nevertheless, we had driven quite a distance to see her so it would have been unfair of me to dismiss her straight away. The owner tacked her up for me and led her to the manège. I mounted her and squeezed her with my legs and began walking. I squeezed her again and she broke into a trot, then I brought her back into walk.

She was nice to ride, very responsive and a lovely pace, although too many unnecessary pieces of additional tack for my liking, which is always a little off-putting because it brings into question whether the horse does need them for reasons an owner is not telling you, or is it just because an owner isn't really in the know about how to use them?

My heart was telling me to take her home there and then but my head was telling me that sadly she was not really what I was looking for. I needed a horse much more solid and slightly bigger if I was going to be long-distance riding. We thanked her owner and said we'd let her know our thoughts later that day. Julie and I had a chat on our drive home and we were both of the same opinion.

A week went by and I spent hours trawling through adverts offering horses for sale. I spotted a second horse I wanted to look at. The description sounded quite positive although there wasn't a picture. This did put me off a little. As we drove into the yard to see her, we spotted a horse tied up outside the stable in front of us and I'm afraid it was one of those moments when your heart sinks and you hope this is not the one you have come to see. Sadly, it was. Out of politeness we went through the motions but again she was not for me. I was not sure what part of her was Arabian?

By now the weeks were turning into months and I was looking at all the advertisements daily, both new and old, for my perfect horse. There was one particular advert I kept coming back to time and time again but it was very brief, only two lines long and there was no picture. The advert simply read: 'Bay Arab mare 14.2 hands. Low mileage, needs bringing back into work following maternity leave'. After my last encounter, I did not really want to go and have a look at a horse unless I had seen a picture first. I suppose it was out of desperation and curiosity I decided to view this third horse (being the one with the brief advert and lack of picture). On this occasion, I took my sister-in-law with me. We were looking upon this as a day out really and my expectations were low.

When we arrived, disappointment set in again as we were directed to a field housing four Arabian horses – three grey and one light bay mare. It was the mare we had come to see. On first inspection we were faced with an overweight horse in need of a good brush and urgent attention required to her overgrown feet. One was severely pigeon-toed. She had three white socks and an uneven blaze down her nose. She had a long flowing black mane and tail.

It was made apparent that this horse had not been ridden for a few years and with the owner reluctant to ride her, I mounted and asked my sister-in-law to lead her down the lane with me dubiously on board. This mare was extremely forward-going and I felt I had no control over her whatsoever, even though she was not doing anything naughty. She was the offspring of a pure-bred Arabian and a Dutch square pacer so with this combination, she moved with an incredibly quick action. She would be perfect for endurance riding! We returned to the yard and I dismounted. I had taken a camcorder with me and asked my sister-in-law to trot the mare up and down the yard whilst I filmed her. She just floated with an amazing action I could have watched her all day. Her beautiful long black mane and tail swayed as she moved and the way she carried her head so proudly! I was captivated.

I was completely torn at that moment. Everything was screaming 'no she's not right for me.' She was extremely forward-going and was definitely not going to be bombproof or a quiet ride but I was completely drawn in by her beauty and action. The very persistent owner could see I was torn and although at that point I was going to go home and think about it, she took control of the situation and offered me a loan to see how I got on with the mare. I thanked her for the offer and said I would give this some consideration but really my head was telling me 'No'.

After returning home, I found myself watching the video of this beautiful mare, over and over again. Her movement was mesmerising. Before I knew it, I found myself making arrangements for a second viewing. This time I would take my husband and Julie.

Julie could see how attached I was too and could see the potential, the key feature being this mare was like a blank canvas. She had been turned away not long after backing and had not done anything since. Although she was rising nine years old, it was a big plus we knew her full history.

My husband, on the other hand, thought I was losing my mind to even consider 'spending money and investing time in such a tatty horse' – his words not mine. Mind you, he had made his feelings very clear from the start, he thought I was bonkers looking to buy a horse when Julie had three horses and she was happy for me to ride them for free!

Well, I came to a decision and made the call. Breeze would be coming the next day on loan!

With my husband still not convinced and with work not yet complete on the stables and land at the new house, I would have to find Breeze a new home quickly. With all systems go, I began making local enquiries, luckily there were plenty of options to choose from near our home. I found a great livery yard a short distance away which offered excellent facilities. It was a lovely big stable within an American barn, an indoor and outdoor school with great hacking potential. Bedding, hay and hard feed were all purchased from the yard so they were items I could cross off my growing list of necessities. Next stop was the local tack shop to acquire new buckets, hay nets, headcollar, lead rope and brushes.

I now had all the essentials covered so it was back home for a sleepless night wondering if I had done the right thing. Could I remember how to care for a horse? Had I realised what a huge commitment I was making? Would I have the time? All these questions were going round and round in my head. It was too late to have second thoughts now as morning arrived.

I headed off to the yard to prepare Breeze's stable. Fresh deep bed down, hay net full of fresh hay, clean water in place and feed purchased. All done. I could do no more now than to wait for Breeze to arrive!

Chapter 3

I was waiting at the stables as I watched the car and trailer pull up into the yard. I could see Breeze, her head looking over the open top door. She was such a stunning mare. The car came to a standstill, the driver's door opened and her owner got out. She walked to the side ramp and gently lowered it. She untied Breeze, led her down the ramp and handed me the lead rope.

I led Breeze around the yard to stretch her legs. It had been a relatively short journey but she was excited to look around the surroundings and explore her new home. Her owner accompanied me to see Breeze's stable. Breeze was happy to walk straight in and began eating the fresh hay hung up in a large hay net in the corner.

We had agreed a loan with a view for me to buy. I was being loaned a bridle and saddle as part of the agreement. So, with the paperwork signed and the tack transferred to my car, I watched Breeze's owner drive away.

To be honest, this scenario was good for me. Breeze belonged to someone else so if this arrangement didn't work out, I could just take her back. If it was a success, then I would pay for her and she would be mine.

I had mixed emotions. My first thought was, *What do I do with Breeze now?* I stood watching her begin her potential new life with me. A new adventure for us both. She seemed settled so I decided it would be best to leave her for a few hours and return later with my boys when I had collected them from school.

My boys unfortunately do not share my passion for horses. I stood in the school yard eagerly waiting to tell them all about Breeze, hoping they would be excited to see her. As we walked to the car they were only interested in,

'What's for tea?' Tea would have to wait as I was making a trip back to the yard first to make sure Breeze was OK.

We arrived back at the yard and I hurried my boys along to the stable. Breeze was still blissfully munching away on her hay. I filled a second hay net and gave her a bucket containing a scoop of happy hoof for her tea, mixed with a little water. She quickly ate this and went straight back to the hay net. I skipped out, refilled her water bucket then left her in peace. Tomorrow I would be riding her!

After a sleepless night, I was up early, dropped the boys off at school and headed off to the yard to see Breeze. I had arranged for Julie to meet me there.

Breeze was clearly not fazed by her new home. She was resting in her stable and approached the door when she saw me. I gave her a bucket of Happy Hoof for breakfast then proceeded to brush her. She looked like she had not been brushed in a while. Her coat was a mixture of her old winter coat with her new summer coat coming through. It was quite dull and matted in places. She was not keen on being brushed and actually continued her dislike of this for many years to come. Her feet were overgrown and in desperate need of a trim. She had never been shod. It was my intention later that day to book a farrier as soon as possible.

Julie arrived when I was brushing Breeze. Underneath the thick matted hair was a beautiful, shiny, red-coloured coat. Breeze was overweight, which was understandable for a horse who had been out of work for at least four years. She was backed at four years old and hacked out only a handful of times before circumstances for her previous owner changed and she had gone to a new home. This led to Breeze being put out to grass until I came along. At this point I had a green horse on my hands who would need taking back to basics.

The bridle and saddle on loan to me didn't fit Breeze properly, but it would do for now due to the little amount of work we had planned initially for an unfit horse. It was my intention that as soon as I was confident, I would keep her, and new tack would be purchased, including a made-to-measure saddle.

Putting the bridle on Breeze was not an easy task. She was not keen on having it go over her left ear. She would throw her head in the air and it took some gentle talking and taking it slowly to persuade her. Once her bridle was on, I put the saddle on her back and loosely fastened the girth. I put her headcollar back on over her bridle and clipped a lead rope to it.

Julie held the lead rope and I proceeded to mount. I gathered up my reins, tightened up the girth and adjusted my stirrups. Julie led Breeze around the yard. Breeze was lively and unlike any horse I had ridden previously! Julie kept a tight hold of the lead rope and Breeze felt like she was going to explode beneath me! Arabs do have a reputation for being spooky so I should have been prepared. We were dealing with an extremely green horse in unfamiliar surroundings, so we were cautious at this stage. We then swapped over and Julie mounted her whilst I led. After twenty minutes or so, we decided that was enough for today. We had achieved what we set out to do so we took her back to her stable, untacked her, settled her with some fresh hay whilst we devised an action plan to get her fit.

First of all, Breeze needed her first ever set of shoes. Calls were made to numerous farriers; I began to panic a little as they all had full books and were not taking on new customers. One I spoke to said although he couldn't take me on, he could give me the name of a local farrier who had just qualified and was setting up a customer base. I gratefully took down Nathen's details.

Nathen would become my farrier for many years in the future and a great farrier too, so a big thank you to him.

I was nervous about her being shod as I had no idea if she would behave herself. Her feet were overgrown and had not seen a farrier for a while, this was evident. However,

Nathen was brilliant with her and she was no problem. She stood still and obliged him each time he picked a foot up. She was hot shod and did not mind the smell of burning hoof or the smoke from it.

With her shoes on, attention now turned to our plan to get Breeze fit. Julie was going to be coming back to the yard after tea that evening to discuss this and would be bringing her husband Bill to meet Breeze. However, nobody could have predicted what we would find when we met at the yard…

Chapter 4

I was so excited at the thought of showing Breeze off to Bill. I went to the stables early to muck out and feed her and waited for my visitors to arrive. As I approached her stable, I couldn't see her. Breeze was lying down when I looked over her door. I hadn't seen her lying down before and she looked so cute. I opened the door and went in expecting her to jump to her feet but she did not move. I put a headcollar on her and tried to coax her to stand. Reluctantly, she was soon on her feet but the untouched hay net was an indication there was something not right. At that point I decided to call the vet just as Julie and Bill arrived.

Whilst we were waiting for the vet, it became apparent Breeze had colic. I put this possibly down to her change of management. She had been living outside twenty-four seven for years and was now being kept in stables twenty-four seven. As with most yards in our area at this time of year, turnout in wet muddy fields during spring was not really an option. Perfectly understandable if farmers/land owners are to preserve grazing and to let the grass grow ready for the summer months.

I led Breeze around the yard until the vet arrived and after an examination, confirmed that it was colic. With a dose of liquid paraffin and instructions for the next twenty-four hours, the vet left and I settled myself in for a night at the stables so I could keep an eye on her. Julie and Bill nipped home and came back, bringing a rug for Breeze. So far, I hadn't bought any rugs and none came with her so I would have to make shopping for rugs a priority. I phoned my husband and updated him on what had been going on for the past few hours and told him I planned to spend the night monitoring Breeze. He arrived an hour or so later with a meat and potato pie, a flask of coffee and a blanket for me. It was going to be a long night.

I was not happy leaving Breeze in case she had another bout of colic during the night. I was also fully aware that she was not my horse and although I would treat her as if she was mine, I felt extra pressure and an extra duty of care because she did belong to someone else.

Breeze was on strict nil by mouth at that point, so when she started eating her straw bed, another call to the vet resulted in me having to remove her from her stable and tie her up in the yard. She was under cover and wrapped in the fleece I had borrowed from Julie. With that, I went to get my car from the parking area and drove into the deserted yard and parked a few feet away from where Breeze was tethered. With her in my line of sight I reclined my seat slightly and attempted to get some sleep in the car.

It was a long, cold night. I spent most of it in my car trying to snatch an hour of sleep here and there whilst keeping an eye on Breeze. My eyes were drawn to a large hole in the stone at the bottom of the barn wall and I hoped I wouldn't be seeing any visitors using it. Sure enough, a huge rat appeared through it, scurrying past Breeze. If there's one thing I can't stand, it's rats! There's never just one either. Each time I got out of the car to go up to Breeze I found myself standing on a bucket just in case!

For the remaining hours of the night there were no more signs of colic thankfully, or rats!

Morning arrived and I was exhausted. The first issue I had to deal with before I could do anything was to remove all the straw from the stable and replace it with shavings. This was a huge task as there must have been at least five bales of straw in there and it was all clean. What a waste, I thought. It took me several hours to sort it all out and it certainly added to the already huge muck heap. At least Breeze seemed to be back to normal and she was able to have a small hay net. By late morning I found myself happy to leave her and I drove home. The house was empty. John had gone to work and our boys were at school, so I made myself a quick cup of tea and crawled into bed for a few hours. Unfortunately, any plans to ride her had been pushed back by a week.

The rest of that week was pretty uneventful. I had Breeze in a routine, while juggling work and family life. I was enjoying loaning a horse, although I hadn't realised how much time this would take each day and that was without factoring in any time to ride.

As we went into the second week, colic struck again. With another vet visit and another dose of liquid paraffin, it became apparent I needed to move her to another yard with some kind of turnout. Keeping her stabled twenty-four hours a day was not working. She needed some grass, no matter how limited.

I spent a few days making enquiries and visiting other yards to look at facilities suitable for Breeze and soon found a yard with a vacancy which offered the turn-out Breeze needed. We would be moving soon.

My thoughts now turned to whether I would continue to loan her or buy her. I was well aware her owner could actually request her back at any point and as I'd grown attached to Breeze already, I didn't want this to potentially happen.

I had a two-week holiday abroad coming up shortly and really wanted this to be a done deal before I went. I had a chat with her owner and we agreed a purchase price which was subject to Breeze passing a five-star vetting for endurance purposes.

I phoned the vet to arrange this. On the morning of the vetting, I was nervous.

What would I do if she failed? At this point I really didn't want to part with her so I was anxious as the vet visit loomed.

It was the first vetting I had requested. In years gone by, I didn't know anyone who had a horse vetted or if this had even been an option. I was already finding out times had changed quite dramatically from twenty-five years ago in many ways.

As the vet arrived, I led Breeze into the yard. We watched him get out of his car and cross the yard to approach us. He was called Mark. Little did we know that day how much we would come to know Mark and how much more he would feature in our lives in the future.

This examination probably took around an hour but felt like a lifetime. Mark would write his findings down and not say much to me unless it was an instruction, for example, to trot up for a reflex test etc. As Breeze had been with me a few weeks, there was no need to have the blood tests completed. I believe this is to establish if a horse has been given anything to either calm it down or mask pain by possibly unscrupulous sellers. Heartbreaking to believe there are people out there who would do this. As Breeze hadn't been ridden much, I didn't feel confident enough to ride her for that part of the test so she was lunged instead. One of the girls on the yard agreed to do for this for me. Breeze soon got the idea of what was expected of her as she circled round the manège, bucking and snorting! This definitely got her heart rate up.

By the end, my heart was in my mouth as I waited for Mark to complete his report before advising me that in his opinion, she was fit for endurance and had passed her vetting. I was so happy I could have cried. I honestly don't know what I would have done if she had failed. It would have been pointless paying out good money for a vetting if I had disregarded the report and bought her anyway. Luckily, I wasn't faced with that dilemma!

By the end of the week, I had returned the borrowed tack and paid the agreed purchase price for Breeze and she was officially mine. It was time to move her to the new yard before I went off on holiday for two weeks. I had been looking forward to this holiday for ages, it had been booked long before I began looking to buy a horse. But I was already looking forward to coming back from it to start some serious riding on her to begin her endurance career.

There was just one more shopping trip required before our holiday and it wasn't for holiday clothes. It was for new tack for Breeze. I also made an appointment for a saddle fitter to come out to us to make sure I purchased a correctly fitted saddle, then it was off to the tack shop for a new bridle, bit and a selection of rugs.

With the new tack and the new yard only a few miles away, the plan was to ride her there. I decided to set off very early on the Saturday morning as part of the journey would be on a busy road and I had not ridden her through any traffic at this point, so had no idea how she would react. My husband walked alongside her.

The roads were quiet and I was enjoying riding her again. She was such a fast walker with her head held high and ears forward. We turned onto the lane and I trotted the last half a mile. She felt great and clearly loved being out somewhere different.

We headed to her new stable, first of all to untack her and put her headcollar on. The plan was to turn her out with her new friends and release her in a big field full of grass.

I led her to the field and opened the gate. She was really excited as I removed her headcollar and let her go. She galloped to the group of horses at the bottom of the enormous field then I watched in horror as they chased her and she went back for more. I knew this would happen as horses are pack animals and have to establish who's in charge. I watched her out-run them all time and time again though; I was so proud of her. She was stunning when she moved, she seemed to float with her beautiful long black tail held high and her beautiful long, flowing black mane.

After watching her for a while she settled down and began grazing. I went home feeling all was going well and planned a ride on her the next day.

The following day I was up early and back at the yard. Breeze had spent the night out in the field with twenty or so other horses. Armed with my headcollar and a carrot I opened the gate and went into the field. I could see Breeze happily grazing as I approached her with a carrot in one hand and the headcollar and lead rope in the other. She took the carrot and as I went to put the head collar on her, she turned her back on me and galloped down the field! I walked down the field, which in size was approximately forty acres! As I approached her again, she galloped away from me back up the field. By now all the horses were joining in. This game went on for around an hour when it became apparent riding her today was not going to happen. She was enjoying her new-found freedom too much. By now I was worn out and totally fed up. Having this horse was not going to plan at all. I was beginning to think I had made a mistake as I headed home.

After lunch I went back to the yard and this time, armed with a bucket of pony nuts, I made my way back down the field. I soon realised this was a bad idea as I shook the bucket and twenty plus horses made their way to me, including Breeze, who got chased away by a grumpy big old grey horse.

I was determined not to give up so I abandoned the bucket and headed back towards Breeze with a handful of nuts and a lead rope. This time I was lucky. As she ate the nuts from my hand, I used my other hand to slide the rope around her neck. She tried to pull away but I had a tight grip. I put her headcollar on and led her from the field, through the yard and into her stable.

After a quick brush, I tacked her up and mounted. She stood still whilst I gathered my reins and waited for my friend to ride in front of me on her bomb-proof schoolmaster. We set off for a short hack as by this time it was getting late. I was also aware Breeze was overweight and would need gently bringing back into work. I was looking forward to getting her fit and ready for her first pleasure ride.

I then went on my two-week holiday abroad; it flew by and I was excited to return home to see Breeze. She had been well-looked after in my absence, although she had had another bout of colic and another vet visit. This time, my poor sister-in-law ended up spending a full night at the stables with her. I'd hoped we had seen the last of the colic now Breeze was out grazing full-time so it was not good to hear she'd been ill again. This was three times now in as many weeks.

She seemed well on my return so I picked up with her pretty much where I had left off.

I loved riding her, she had a fantastic pace being out of a Dutch square pacer. The Arab in her shone through too with her spooky, flighty ways. I had to have my wits about me to ride her, she was definitely not a novice ride.

After a successful Sunday afternoon hack, I turned Breeze out for the night and went home for tea.

I had barely been home for an hour before I received a call from one of the girls from the yard.

'You need to come back quickly, Breeze has colic, I found her in the field rolling around and have brought her up to the yard.'

I ran out of the house and got into my car and drove back to the yard to find Breeze being walked around by one of the girls. She had been spotted rolling continuously in the field, getting up then getting back down again, looking at her flanks – classic signs.

I phoned the vet again. This would be the fourth visit for colic in a matter of weeks.

By the time he arrived it was becoming clear a dose of liquid paraffin was not going to do the trick this time.

An examination and injection seemed to help as Breeze got to her feet. It was looking like I would be spending another night at the stables.

A few hours passed and the clock ticked towards midnight.

Then the realisation of the seriousness of the situation began to set in.

Breeze was down on the floor, sweating and making noises I never want to hear again and going downhill fast right before my eyes.

Events were about to take a turn for the worse.

Chapter 5

I called the vet again. It seemed to take forever waiting for him to return, although it was just under an hour. It was Mark, who'd carried out the vetting weeks before.

He took one look at her and said, 'She needs to go to Leahurst now.' Leahurst is the Philip Leverhulme Equine Hospital at the University of Liverpool.

As Mark phoned ahead, I called my husband in a blind panic. We didn't have a trailer; where were we going to get one from at 1 am? Neither did we have a car with a tow bar on it. So not only did we need a trailer immediately, we needed a car to pull it. We were so lucky to have great friends who lived next door to the yard, one of whom was Simon, who instantly offered the use of his trailer and his vehicle to tow it.

John arrived back in the yard with the trailer ready to go and Mark managed to get Breeze to her feet. We hoped and prayed she would load. Just to be on the safe side, Mark gave her a light sedative to make her comfortable and thankfully she made her way up the ramp and into the trailer without any hesitation. With her secure, we set off on the hour-long drive.

With my husband driving and with me sat beside him, we went along the empty dark roads in silence. I was numb and in disbelief, how could it be that within six weeks my dream appeared to be shattering before my eyes.

As we pulled up into the yard at Leahurst a number of staff in green overalls rushed over to help us. To be honest, most of it was a blur that night and still is. I don't remember who took Breeze out of the trailer but she was taken away for an examination whilst I stood in a daze. John and I were ushered into a nearby waiting room. I remember sitting there in silence when a veterinary nurse approached me carrying a clip board with an authorisation form on it she wanted me to sign. She was trying to explain that Breeze needed to go to surgery immediately. The severity of the situation was she would probably die without surgery and with there being a high risk of losing a horse during colic surgery there was no guarantee she would survive it either, she was so poorly.

I burst into tears and remember being asked if I'd owned her for a long time. 'Only six weeks,' I blurted out though my tears.

I took told of the pen and signed the form knowing this treatment would cost thousands and at the end of it I might have a dead horse, but I didn't care, I had to give her a fighting chance.

With there being nothing more we could do, we were advised to go home as it would be several hours before we would know if the surgery had been a success.

With Breeze's life hanging in the balance, we left Leahurst at 3am. It was nearly 4am when we arrived home and got into bed. By now I was both physically and emotionally drained. As my husband and I lay in bed it was impossible to sleep. We were waiting for a phone call, which finally came around 5am. I heard the phone ringing and wanted to hide from it, so I covered my head with the duvet. Pathetic, I know, a ringing phone cannot harm you but I was dreading what the outcome of answering it would be.

John answered it and all I recall was him saying an odd word every now and then like 'OK' or 'right', then he ended with, 'Thanks for letting me know.' He put the phone down and turned to me. I peered from under the duvet holding my breath. My heart was in my mouth waiting for him to tell me what had just been said. Basically, Breeze was out of surgery but was by no means out of the woods yet. She was still very poorly. Once the surgeon had opened her up, he found her small intestine was absolutely riddled with tapeworms; this meant a large part of her intestine had to be removed. Although I had wormed her during the six weeks I had owned her, it would never have been enough to kill off the size of the huge infestation she already had, so surgery was only ever going to have been the only option at this stage and the only option to save her life. All we could do now was wait.

As John went to work later than morning, I took the boys to school wondering what events would transpire that day. I was dreading the day ahead.

I returned home and sat in the kitchen staring at the clock on the wall, watching the hours slowly tick by.

I phoned Leahurst later that day for an update and was told pretty much the same thing. Breeze was in intensive care and being watched around the clock. I knew she was in safe hands now so all I could do was wait and pray.

We got through Monday night and I was given permission to go and see her on Tuesday afternoon. I finished work at lunchtime and drove the sixty-mile round trip to go and visit her.

I don't think Breeze recognised me, why would she? I had only been in her life six weeks and it wasn't going well so far. She was in a stable, with a drip attached to her mane with the bag of fluid hanging from the ceiling. She just stood there with an empty look in her eyes. I could do nothing more but talk to her, telling her she would be OK.

As the week passed, she was getting stronger and stronger, and during my Thursday visit I was given the good news! She was out of the woods and well enough to go home.

She was painfully thin, having dropped a considerable amount of weight. Only weeks before I was faced with how to manage an overweight horse to now trying to manage an underweight one.

I woke up Friday morning, very excited and a little apprehensive. I knew this was going to be a long road to recovery, but at least we were lucky to have the opportunity. We once again had to call upon Simon for his vehicle and trailer, and will be eternally grateful to him for his help. We drove to Leahurst and pulled up into the yard. Within the hour, armed with all my instructions and with Breeze loaded in the trailer, we were on our way home. It was heaven to see her back in her stable, munching hay and looking content. The first stage of her long road to recovery would be eight weeks of box rest with a ten-minute walk out in hand to graze once or twice a day. She had a neatly stitched wound along her abdomen which would need bathing twice daily.

She was fine on the Friday but upon my return back to her on Saturday morning she was clearly not at all well. Her hay net was still full from the night before and even though rugged up she was shivering uncontrollably. I rang Leahurst immediately and they told me to bring her back.

Breeze would spend another agonising three days at Leahurst before she was well enough again to return home to continue box rest.

The following weeks rolled along as we got into a daily routine. I would see her before I went to work. I would clean her wound, skip out, feed her, fill her hay net and give her fresh water, then I would walk her in hand to graze for ten minutes. She was a good patient and happy to stay in her stable because there were other horses stabled next to her and across from her, so she had lots of company.

I would pick my sons up from school in the afternoon and go back to the stables and carry out the same routine.

On one of these afternoons, I asked my son James, who was twelve at the time, to lead Breeze to the grass and I would come and get her from him once her stable was ready. I told him not to take her out of the yard and not to let go of her lead rope. Famous last words.

I finished getting her stable ready and was just about to go and find James and take Breeze off him when one of the girls ran into the yard shouting my name. I ran out shouting, 'What's the matter?'

'You need to come quick, there's been an accident, somebody beeped a car horn at James and Breeze, she spooked and ran, James fell over, didn't let go of the lead rope and he's been dragged along by her.'

James had taken her out of the yard and onto the lane.

At that point, I saw Breeze being led into the yard by one of the girls, with a distraught James walking beside her with blood all over his hands, lip and head. With offers of help to look after Breeze, I put James straight into the car and we headed off to casualty.

Chapter 6

Luckily the hospital was only a twenty-minute drive away and once there James was thankfully assessed pretty quickly. His injuries looked worse than they first appeared to be. He had cuts and bruises to his head and lips and three-degree rope burns to both hands.

Once treated, we were home within a couple of hours and exhausted, so we all headed off to bed.

I lay awake all night.

Owning a horse again was not something I was enjoying at all. In fact, so far, it felt like a bad dream I could not wake up from. It was nothing but hard work and heartache. I was beginning to think I'd made a big mistake. Within a couple of months, I now owned a sick horse I couldn't ride, had huge vet's bills running into the thousands and now one of my children had been injured too.

James soon recovered and I continued with the daily routine until the eight weeks came to an end and Breeze moved into the next phase of her recovery; eight weeks of daily small paddock turnout.

My next challenge was where to turn her out. The paddock needed to be around eight times the size of her stable. With this facility not available at the yard we moved to Plan B – create the paddock on the land next to our new house.

The renovation works at the house were going well but the property was nowhere near ready for us to move into and the stables and paddocks were not ready for Breeze. Suddenly her moving became a priority.

Fencing was ordered and my husband and his dad spent all weekend creating paddocks on the four acres of land to split it into two two-acre turnout areas. Once done, a small paddock was then created in one of them for Breeze to go into now to recover. Then work had to be done to the stables. They had not been touched for years and needed clearing of rubbish and the rotted wooden stable doors needed replacing. It was a mammoth task to do in the time frame we had, and it had not been our intention to start any of this until we had actually moved into the house first.

I was looking forward to moving her because although we wouldn't be living at the new house for a while, our current home was only around the corner so I was nearer her anyway. With everything in place and her stable looking amazing, it was time for her to move.

We decided to move her early on the Saturday morning before the roads became busy.

John and I would lead her together. It was just under a mile.

We expected her to be really giddy as it was the first time she had been out properly for over two months.

The roads were quiet and it was a beautiful sunny August morning so it was a lovely morning to walk.

I was very conscious that it had only been eight weeks since Breeze's major surgery and she was now barefoot. It had been my intention to keep her very first set of shoes, which had only been on her feet a couple of weeks, but they had been removed and discarded at Leahurst. The road didn't seem an issue for her to be barefoot as she walked along nicely.

In fact, she was loving being out and I was very happy with her progress.

As we walked onto our own yard, she was looking at her surroundings and called out to a couple of horses in the paddock adjoining ours. I led her straight into her stable. She wouldn't be turned out today, today was all about settling her in, she had done enough for one day. She went straight to the hay net and began happily munching away.

Occasionally she would put her head over the door, circle around the deep bedded shavings then go back to the hay.

All was going well so far so we decided to head off and leave her for a few hours to settle in. So far so good.

We headed back to the old yard to collect our car and clear out her old stable, then headed home for lunch.

Later that afternoon I went back to our new house to check on progress and Breeze. It would be almost a year before we would move into the house and be near her, but that wasn't a problem at all. For the first time since I'd bought her she was only around the corner from us, so it was an ideal situation.

The following morning, I decided it was time to start the next phase of her recovery programme – small paddock turnout for the next eight weeks for a couple of hours a day. I was very nervous about doing this. Even though her scar from her surgery was looking fine and healing nicely it was still crucial at this stage that she did not go off bucking and galloping around.

The small paddock we had created for her was an ideal size and not big enough for her to build up any momentum, or so I thought!

I had already been in touch with our vet and was in possession of an oral calming product to give her the day of her first turnout. Once this had been given to her in her mouth by syringe, I waited about half an hour for it to get into her system then led her to the paddock. I left her headcollar on and unclipped the lead rope. Well, that was it! She went off like a bat out of hell, bucking and taking up every inch of the space. She had realised my worst fears.

I panicked and climbed into the paddock as quickly as I could to catch her. Luckily, she gave me a second to grab hold of her headcollar and I managed to clip the lead rope on quickly and stop her in her tracks. Clearly the adrenalin rush far outweighed the sedative.

I let her graze for half an hour or so before leading her back to the stable. That was enough excitement for one day.

Over the next few days, I continued leading her to the paddock and kept her on the lead rein so she could graze a couple of times a day until I was confident she was calm enough to be turned out on her own. She would then spend all day in the small paddock then back in the stable overnight. We soon got into a routine and I was very pleased with her.

As the next eight weeks passed it was time to start the third and final phase of her recovery. This was obviously the part I had been looking forward to over the past four months since this nightmare had begun. It was time to get back in the saddle and start to ride her!

As with all the stages it would be small steps. My first intention was to tack her up and sit on her back and if she felt OK with this, I would just go up and down the yard for ten minutes. My biggest fear was that she might buck!

Chapter 7

Breeze stood happily in her stable with her head over the door and her ears forward. I had given her a brush, which she always hated, especially being brushed on her head and even more so around her ears. I put her bridle on then approached her slowly with her saddle. I placed it on her back and gently pulled up the girth and at this point kept a very light contact. I led her up and down the yard a couple of times before tightening the girth to see what she made of it. Whilst the girth wasn't near the long scar she had from surgery; I wasn't sure if any pressure might affect it. She was a good as gold though and didn't flinch at all.

It was time to bite the bullet and mount her. My heart was in my mouth at the thought of being dumped on the yard! I actually had no reason to believe she would do this other than concerns she may have uncomfortable twinges from the surgery, which may be aggravated by weight on her back. She had also developed a small hernia. Bearing in mind I had owned her for such a short length of time, of which the majority I had spent nursing her from death's door, I really couldn't call how this was going to pan out. I fastened my hat, put my gloves on and led her out to the mounting block.

With a final tightening of the girth, I put my left foot in the stirrup and gently lifted my right leg over the saddle and sat on her, talking to her all the time, trying not to let her feel my anxiety.

I gently squeezed her with my heels and asked her to 'walk on' and she obliged beautifully.

It felt amazing to be back in the saddle and I could have happily sat there all day but knew I could only be on her back for ten minutes that day.

The following weeks rolled into months and Breeze and I progressed well together. She was getting stronger every day and I finally dared to believe we might have a future together. We had several loops to ride around where we lived which were ideal for building her strength up with plenty of hills, lanes and some roads so she could get used to traffic.

With Christmas and the New Year out of the way we looked ahead at starting our endurance journey together.

Our first outing would be a ten-mile pleasure ride around Derbyshire's beautiful Hope Valley. This remained one of my favourite rides due to the breath-taking scenery and its proximity to my home.

I had done several pleasure rides alongside Julie, with me riding Belle, so had an idea of what to expect and was looking forward to seeing how Breeze reacted to long distances. Julie and Bill, both being advanced endurance riders, had years of experience so I would be in good hands with them to learn the ropes.

I had built Breeze up to this ride with Julie's help. Julie and Bill had been my support network since Breeze had come into my life. I couldn't have got this far without them.

We had already changed my convertible car for a 4x4 by now and I felt I needed my own trailer. I mentioned the subject to John and he questioned if we needed to buy one. At this point we had been borrowing a trailer from my sister-in-law and renting one from a local company. This was great but not as convenient as being able to load up anytime and go out anywhere at a moment's notice.

John agreed we could go and look at second-hand trailers – 'But we're not buying one today,' he said.

Off we went to a well-known dealership to look at a vast number of trailers. To cut a long story short, from the difference in price between second-hand and brand-new trailers, we actually came away having ordered a brand-new special edition black trailer which we collected the following weekend! It was John who got more carried away than I did making this decision!

So much for him being adamant about not buying one!

On the morning of the ride, John attached the trailer to the car and drove it onto the yard and I began to gather my list of necessary items we would need for the day. It was early spring and the weather was good.

We had packed that much stuff John thought we were going for a week. The main items were bridle, saddle, feed, water, hay net, boots, spare headcollar and rope, muck bucket and shovel, and for myself, hat, gloves, boots, a couple of different jackets, drinks and sandwiches. I'm sure we had much more than this packed as it seemed to take forever to unload it all when we got home!

We arrived at the venue early and gained a good parking spot. Breeze travelled well and was eager to be unloaded. I walked her around to stretch her legs until it was time to tack up and head out.

Julie and I went to the official tent to register and collect our numbered bibs. We then tacked our horses up and left John and Bill walking them around whilst Julie and I got ready to ride.

All ready to go, we mounted, tightened our girths and went to leave the venue and ride out onto the lane.

I was apprehensive to see what Breeze would do if horses passed her. Would she try to follow them? Would I be able to stop her? What would she do if we caught up to horses in front of her? Julie and I had set off when we saw a gap in other horses going out. Breeze was raring to go and soon carrying me at her fantastic extended trotting pace.

I felt that finally, after a year, we were starting the journey together which I had hoped for since the day I'd first set eyes on Breeze. It had been one hell of a journey so far and not in a good way.

We had an amazing ride through the beautiful Derbyshire countryside. The ride was mainly though undulating tracks and fields. We only saw a handful of riders as we managed to stay ahead. We had some beautiful canters on funnelled areas and before we knew it, we were back at the venue. Breeze was in her element, she loved being out somewhere different. This clearly was her forte.

Once back at the venue, we untacked and got ready to take her home. She walked into the trailer quite happily and as we headed back home, I had a huge smile on my face. I'd never thought this day would come after what she and I had already been through together.

Next step would be entering a twenty-five-mile competitive ride!

This event was only a few weeks away so it gave me a chance to keep Breeze's fitness level up by riding the beautiful long trails near home. She always loved going out on long rides and always amazed me by her memory. She would notice anything which appeared at the side of the road or lane today that wasn't there yesterday and generally spook at it!

She would never be a horse you could ride without having your wits about you as she could turn on a pinhead and have you off in a flash. I loved her quirky ways.

With training going well, the day arrived for our first competitive ride… Ackworth Moor Top.

Chapter 8

It was a long drive to Ackworth Moor Top. We set off to the venue early, aiming to be one of the first to head out riding the course. It was a cold morning with the weather forecast not looking great for the day ahead. We had attached the trailer to the car the night before and I had packed everything we would need for a competitive ride, including cooler rug and boots for Breeze, extra hay nets full of hay, plenty of sugar beet water, slosh bottles full of water, feeds, change of clothes for me, my hat, gloves and boots, food and drinks for myself and John.

We would be out all day today so had to make sure we were well-prepared for both ourselves and Breeze.

We were expecting this ride to be popular as it was one of the first of the season, but I was hoping we wouldn't end up riding with either a crowd of horses in front of us or behind. I still didn't know what Breeze would be like surrounded by many excitable horses so our aim was to get out riding early and hope not many horses caught us up. This ride had an entry level of a hundred horses and was full.

A pleasure ride is quite different to a competitive ride. This time we would be up against the clock, so a steady speed was vital. We would not be meeting horses today ambling along.

As we pulled into the venue, Julie and Bill were already there. Julie and I went over to the Secretary to register and collect our numbered bibs whilst John and Bill walked the horses around to stretch their legs.

I was lucky to be riding with Julie. She had mapped the course out and knew what time we would have to reach each checkpoint by and the speed we would need to be riding at to achieve it. Next step was to take our horses to the vet for the compulsory pre-ride vetting. Each horse has its heart rate counted at beats per minute, then a trot up to make sure there was no lameness. After this we headed to the farrier to check that the feet were OK. All of the checks were passed and with the paperwork completed and signed, we were good to go.

As I tacked Breeze up she became very excited and I began to feel a little apprehensive. In reality I had no idea what was coming. With Breeze ready, I put my gloves on, slipped my trainers off and pulled on my boots. Last of all I pulled my numbered bib on over my jacket and mounted Breeze whilst John held her reins. I joined Julie then we rode towards the timekeeper heading out of the venue. The timekeeper noted our numbers which were on the front and back of our bibs, wished us a good ride then with the clock now ticking, we rode out of the venue and down the track. There's a window in which you have to complete the ride. Come back too soon you can fail; equally come back too late you can fail. The test is all about keeping up a steady pace, gauging how many miles you've ridden and gauging the time you have left to ride. The timekeeping is only one of many factors though, leading to whether you pass or fail.

As we set off the weather was good, cold but dry. The ride itself was along many tracks and a little roadwork. Breeze was focused and clearly loving being in different surroundings. We headed onto the outskirts of a large field and began a great long canter. We soon caught up with a group of riders up ahead and with permission to pass, headed into the forest on a narrow winding track. Still keeping up the pace, we had to duck low against the horses' necks as the branches were too low for us to sit up in our saddles. I lay against Breeze's neck, putting my full trust in her to keep going as I couldn't see a thing! She continued to canter along the winding track whilst the peak on my hat had slipped down over my eyes and I had to wait until we were out of the wooded area and into the clearing before I could push it back up and gather myself back into position on my saddle.

We trotted over a road crossing and saw our crew ahead, John and Bill waiting at the first checkpoint. Bill handed Julie a slosh bottle and John handed me mine, we tipped this up and down the horses' necks to cool them down then they offered both horses a welcome drink of sugar beet water. Finally, with us both being handed a bottle of drinking water each, Julie and I took a sip and then we were on our way again within seconds.

After around ten miles, the heavens opened and the rain came down heavily. But we continued at a strong pace throughout.

After more tracks and farmland, we came to the next checkpoint and a quick meet-up again with our crew and followed the same procedure as before.

By now, I was struggling to carry on with the rising trot. I was not used to keeping up this speed for miles, my legs were starting to feel like lead weights and I was bouncing all over the place on Breeze's back. Luckily, she was not fazed one bit. She was clearly born to do this.

We passed another group of horses ahead and by now the rain had stopped. We were soaked to the skin. My wet gloves were sticking to my reins and my jodhpurs felt really heavy as they clung to my legs.

The ride took us just short of three and a half hours, which was perfect timing. We trotted back into the venue past the timekeeper, who recorded our finish time. I had a huge smile on my face. This was what I had bought Breeze to do and with our setbacks over the past twelve months, we had finally completed our first competitive ride.

I walked Breeze back to the trailer, dismounted, took her tack off, put her headcollar on and began walking her round to cool off. We had a window of thirty minutes to cool down the horses and go back to the vet for the final vetting which would tell us if we had successfully ridden the course and either passed or failed. By now it was raining again but the horses were still warm. The key now was to slosh them with cold water to bring down their heart rates and keep them moving to avoid them stiffening up.

As we headed to the vet, Breeze seemed really chilled. Her heart beats per minute were recorded and we completed a trot up and down again. The vet sheet was then taken to the Secretary for completion. We would have to wait now to see if we had completed all of the elements of the ride satisfactorily and if so, what grade we had achieved.

We rugged up both Breeze and Belle and gave them a small feed. Then we let them graze.

Julie and I headed back to the Secretary to collect our results and hand back our numbered bibs. The best I was hoping for, for my first ever competitive ride, was at least a completion; but I was absolutely over the moon to find we had achieved a Grade 1, this being the highest grade. It meant we had completed the ride at the perfect speed, Breeze's heart rate was low both in and out and she was fit at the end. Not only this, when the ride results were published a few weeks later by Endurance GB, Breeze and I had achieved first place in the Novice Group!

To this day, that was and still is my favourite ride on Breeze, I loved everything about the day. It had been a real test of endurance for us both, but to come out of it as we did made me believe we had great prospects of getting to Advanced Level. I was absolutely over the moon.

We would need to complete one more ride of at least twenty-five miles to move from Novice to Open Level, then one forty-mile ride and one of fifty miles to move from Open Level to Advanced Level. With determination it was doable for this to be achieved this season.

We loaded Breeze back into our trailer and she happily munched on her hay net as we made the long journey back home. I slept all the way! It had been a long, exhausting day but I'd enjoyed every single minute.

Once home, I turned her out in the paddock, watched her get straight down for a roll then get up and start grazing whilst we started the arduous task of unpacking everything, along with plenty of wet clothes, numnah, rugs and muddy boots. All this washing would have to wait until tomorrow.

The plan would now be to rest Breeze the following week then start training for the next twenty-five-mile ride which was a month away at The Eld.

Chapter 9

Soon it was time for the next competitive ride. Breeze had been given a week off following Ackworth Moor Top, then the following two weeks we had hacked out locally and just done some gentle rides. She was already fit so it was just a case of keeping this maintained. She was like a different horse to the one we had brought back from Leahurst. She had gained weight and was just right now and her muscles were also toned.

Again, as with Ackworth Moor Top, the Eld ride was a couple of hours' drive away to the venue and another twenty-five-mile ride. It was another very early start with the car and trailer packed again with all the necessary items.

Upon arrival we followed the same process as before. Once vetted, we were tacked up and out on the course before the ride got too busy.

The weather was good and we had some lovely canters along disused rail tracks. We knew there would be an area of water to cross but I wasn't sure just how wide or deep this would be! Several riders ahead of us were stuck at the water with their horses point-blank refusing to cross. There was no way around it, so you were either going through it or going home!

As we approached the water, I had no idea what Breeze would do. I'd never even ridden her through a puddle! I think I expected Breeze to refuse but she stepped into the water and continued as the level passed over her knees and touched the bottom of my stirrups. I lifted my feet up and back towards her flank. We waded across the long deep stretch of water and out of the other side looking back at several horses still refusing to budge.

We carried on passing many things which caused Breeze to spook, mainly crisp packets blowing in the wind, but she seemed really focused until we started cantering along the next wooded area. Suddenly, mid-canter, she stopped dead in her tracks. I landed on her neck sideways and lost my stirrups. I was frantically trying to get back into the saddle whilst my feet at this point were kicking Breeze's rump. She started to buck. In a flash I was catapulted, somersaulting over her head and I landed on my back with a thump on the hard ground. In disbelief and in a daze, I scrambled to my feet. I was sure I hadn't broken any bones but my back was sore. Breeze was grazing nearby.

At this point we were now losing time and had to get a move on. I didn't want to get back on her but was faced with no other choice. We were miles away from anywhere. I mounted as soon as I could and we walked for a minute whilst I gathered myself together. I had no idea what had caused Breeze to behave like she had. There wasn't any time to walk and as I sat on her back she wasn't listening to me at all, she was too hyper. I was holding my reins as tight as I could and for the first time, I could feel myself beginning to panic as I felt she was out of my control.

We crossed a road and headed into a large field. The ride continued on the outskirts of the farmer's field, so we proceeded to canter. I can only assume by now Breeze was just too excited, she raced to catch up with a group of riders she had spotted in the distance. We went round a bend but Breeze went straight into the bushes. We composed ourselves and slowed down and walked for a few minutes to the next checkpoint and I was very happy to see our crew, John and Bill.

I jumped off and announced I was done. My back was hurting, Breeze felt lame and I was in no frame of mind to continue.

We were in the middle of nowhere and as we were still around fifteen miles away from the venue, we needed to call for assistance to collect Breeze and I.

The event was very well-organised and in no time at all, a trailer arrived for us and took us back to the venue. Julie continued the ride. There was little point her day being ruined too.

Once at the venue, Breeze was checked by the vet. She was lame and I was advised to rest her for several weeks once back home. I was very disappointed as after such a high at Ackworth Moor Top, today had ended on an all-time low. We loaded Breeze into our trailer and left her munching on her hay as we had decided to wait for Julie to come in. Next, the heavens opened and the heavy rain came. Julie was still out on the course. We found out later eight riders, including me, had got dumped at the same spot. Apparently, it was deer stalking in the bushes which had caused all these horses to spook.

An hour or so later, we saw Julie and Belle heading towards the timekeeper and back into the venue. We had a chat whilst Julie cooled Belle down and headed to the vet. With Belle then loaded in their box we all set off for home.

John and I drove home in silence. It had been a long day. My back was hurting and I felt mentally drained. I was just setting out on what I was hoping would be a great endurance career for myself and Breeze and we'd had a major setback already.

Breeze was lame and being rested. I called the vet to check her and after a number of scans and X-rays, it was confirmed that she had torn a ligament on her offside back leg. She needed to rest for a minimum of a month, to my dismay.

During this month I didn't ride at all. My back recovered from the bruising but my mind was a long, long way from recovery. All I could think about was her bucking and being so fast and me being unable to control her. The length of time out of the saddle made this worse and escalated my thoughts.

I was relieved when more rest was prescribed for Breeze after the first month as it sadly gave me the excuse I needed not to ride her.

Nearly two months after the Eld Ride, Breeze was ready for light exercise. I was so nervous about riding her, which was crazy after what we had achieved at Ackworth Moor Top. Julie offered to come over and take Breeze out for me. I didn't hesitate to take her up on this offer.

It was a lovely Saturday morning, perfect weather for Breeze's first outing. As Julie arrived, I already had Breeze brushed, tacked up and ready to go.

Julie mounted Breeze whilst I held her. She didn't flinch so we took her on a local walk with me at her side. All good. Breeze was having a good look around but didn't put a foot wrong. Hard to believe she hadn't been ridden for months. No signs of lameness, she was completely recovered.

The plan would be for me to ride her the next day.

Chapter 10

Next morning, I woke up and the thought of riding Breeze filled me with apprehension. I just could not get thoughts of falling off at the Eld out of my mind.

Breeze was not then and never would be a novice ride and I would not have considered myself a novice rider – until today. At this point, the fact I'd ridden her loads of times didn't count for anything.

I went into the stable to get Breeze ready. Once tacked up I led her onto the yard and already I was thinking I just wanted this to be over with. She stood perfectly still as I mounted and composed myself. I gathered my reins, took a deep breath and gently squeezed her to walk on. As we set off, I could feel myself getting more and more anxious, which was obviously feeding through to Breeze.

As I turned the corner, a crisp packet blew towards us and she did what she'd done a thousand times: spooked and spun round. I just lost it completely, I grabbed a handful of her mane, took my feet out of the stirrups and jumped off her as quickly as I could. My behaviour was totally irrational and although I knew it, I just could not change my mindset and I could not bring myself to get back on her.

I was totally used to her spooking, she would just spin round and then stand still, head high in the air, ears forward just looking, frozen on the spot! She was waiting for reassurance to walk on. She didn't try to gallop off out of control, which in my mind is exactly what I envisaged she was going to do now.

I turned around and led Breeze back home, untacked her and turned her out into the field. My behaviour would lead to me relying on Julie to come over every weekend to ride Breeze and later for my husband or Julie to lead me if I was riding.

I would ride because I felt I had to, not because I wanted to and although I still loved horse riding, there was no pleasure in this. I was desperate to break this mindset I had and hoped it would take just one ride to do this as it took only one ride to ruin it.

I drove my husband to the end of his tether on many occasions. He thought I was pathetic. He had seen what Breeze and I were capable of together and the fact he was now leading me around on her drove him to despair. He would come home from work and I would be waiting to ask him to lead me. He just wanted his tea and a sit-down after a long day at work, so he was already agitated before we set off. I couldn't blame him. Once he was leading Breeze, I would be jumping off every five minutes if I saw anything ahead that I thought she would spook at. John would constantly be saying, 'She's not doing anything.' To which I would reply, 'She was going to do this, she was going to do that.'

In the end, after months of this, he said, 'I can't do this anymore, if you're not going to ride her, then you need to sell her.'

At that point, I realised I needed to pull myself together and I started taking Breeze out really early in the morning before anyone else was around or potentially anything around which she could spook at. I would start off leading her then once at the bottom of Coach Road I would psyche myself up to get on her. She always stood still whilst I got on her back and whilst I adjusted her girth. Coach Road was narrow, stony and uphill with trees either side, so there was nowhere for her to take off but uphill, so I felt quite safe. Once at the top I would ride the loop, about an hour altogether from home, a quiet lane and track. We would see an occasional car or tractor, then mostly dog walkers or other riders. I would jump off if I saw anything I thought she might spook at then get back on again when I thought it was safe. It was all still going on in my head but at least I was taking her out on my own which was more than I had done previously.

Julie would still come over to ride and I felt I was getting some confidence back as I began riding more than walking at one point!

Julie suggested a pleasure ride. It sounded like a great idea to take the bull by the horns and just go for it. So we entered in for a ten-mile pleasure ride.

It was June and the day of the ride. At least there was no pressure today. It was not a competitive ride. My hope was that Breeze would be focused and the ride wouldn't be too busy and would be the perfect way to break the cycle I found myself in. I figured once we got going, Breeze would soon settle and my hope was I would get my confidence back as quickly as I'd lost it at the Eld ride.

We arrived at the venue and to my dismay it was really busy. John parked the trailer and I lowered the ramp. Breeze was calling out to horses nearby and was over-excited already.

As I led her out of the trailer, she almost dragged me out. Trying to tack her up was difficult as she was spinning around. John held her tightly and straight away I changed my mind. I did not want to ride but I knew John would go mad if I admitted this after the length of time we had been travelling to get there.

Julie was ready to go, riding Belle. I had no choice but to gather myself together and get on with it.

John held Breeze as I mounted and I asked him just to hold onto her rein and walk with us for a few minutes until she settled down a little.

This was a farm ride and to be fair I didn't realise what that actually meant until we were on it. It was going to be a fast ride as it was on a purpose-built grass track, no roads, so ideal to canter all the way if you wanted to and that's exactly what riders were doing.

Rules still applied, even with a pleasure ride; you have to slow down and ask permission to pass a rider. However, Breeze was hearing hooves coming up behind her and she exploded. Even as riders slowed down to pass, as soon as they did and set off again, Breeze was dying to go after them. I was shouting to Julie as Breeze was bunny-hopping sideways. I jumped off as soon as I could, we had literally only left John a few minutes ago. I was both devastated and annoyed with myself.

By now Breeze was going completely bonkers, spinning me around in circles and calling out. I was struggling to keep hold of her. Every time another horse came anywhere near her, she lost it. I shouted to Julie to carry on. There was no point in her missing out on the ride. We had only just started. I struggled to hang on to Breeze as I desperately tried to get her back to the start. I had my left hand holding both her reins tightly and my right hand firmly on her chest trying to stop her circling me.

I managed to get off the track when a lady saw me struggling and came across to see if I needed any help. She thought I'd fallen off. I explained briefly I was too nervous to ride and Breeze had been a handful. She watched as Breeze was bouncing all over the place with me hanging on for grim death! Sounds extreme but it was how it was! She shouted, 'Would you sell her?'

I shouted back, 'No.'

But she ran towards us and pushed a piece of paper in my pocket with her name and phone number on and said, 'If you change your mind, please call me. My son is an advanced endurance rider and Breeze would be perfect for him. He would not be fazed by her at all.'

I saw John near the car and shouted for him to open the trailer. I wanted to go straight home as soon as possible. I led Breeze straight in then took her tack off and slipped her headcollar on.

With Breeze loaded, the journey back home was silent. John was not happy with me at all and I couldn't blame him. He had been patient with me for months whilst I was behaving irrationally.

As we got near home, I decided it would be best all round if I sold Breeze. I announced this as soon as we pulled up on the driveway. I retrieved the piece of paper which had been pushed into my pocket a few hours earlier, then I made the call as soon as Breeze was back in her stable. I thought I'd be relieved now I'd made the decision but I didn't feel anything but huge disappointment with myself.

We had John's family coming for Sunday lunch and we had to make a start on the food. I just wanted to crawl into bed and pull the duvet over my head, I was so depressed. John didn't know, but his family were coming as we had a great surprise planned for his upcoming special birthday.

I had bought tickets to a boxing match in Las Vegas and the plan was to give him the tickets after lunch, also he and I were going to Las Vegas for a week and his parents were going to look after our boys whilst we were there.

Lunch went well and the anticipation of our surprise focused my mind elsewhere for a while. John was delighted, so the day ended much better than it had started.

I had a sleepless night, as next day Breeze's potential new family were coming up to see her.

They were a lovely family. Breeze would be for their son. He rode her round our loop near home whilst his mum, grandma and sister walked with me. I could see she was perfect for him. He was a great rider, very chilled but in control and Breeze was very responsive to him. He loved her.

I was asked if I would be happy to take her to a competitive event for him to ride Breeze to try her out?

Yes, I was happy with that. I loved to see her out on course as I knew how much she loved it. The ride went well, twenty-five miles. She thrived with him on board and he was absolutely thrilled with her. He rode alongside Julie and we crewed for them. After the ride was over, we loaded Breeze back into the trailer and was asked if I could take Breeze to her new home the following Saturday?

This would give me a final five days with her.

I agreed.

I received a phone call two days before just to confirm all was still OK for Saturday and was advised that Breeze's new stable was ready. The family had been out buying lots of new things for her and were very excited.

I woke up on Friday morning, looked at my husband and said, 'I can't go through with it, I've changed my mind, I can't sell her.'

I expected him to be really annoyed with me but instead he merely said, 'She's your horse, so if you don't want to sell her, don't sell her.'

All day I worried as I knew I had to make the call to let the family down. It had to be done that day as she was supposed to be going the following day.

It was awful. I hate letting anyone down, especially a child. He was devastated. But equally, I couldn't part with Breeze so I just had to put this behind me and move on.

What now? I wasn't going to ride her but I did have a plan for her later in life, which was now going to be an earlier option. I would have her put in foal.

We had a family holiday booked to Kenya, so I would enjoy our holiday then look for a suitable stallion upon my return.

With Breeze being cared for back home and the pressure off me having to ride her, we set off on our Kenyan adventure. I was really looking forward to getting away. John and I had been to Kenya before, years ago before we had our boys. We knew they would love going on safari which is why we chose to return with them. We had a great first week – the hotel, weather, food, everything was amazing. We spent two incredible days out in the Masai Mara and it truly was turning out to be the trip of a lifetime.

As the second week started, we had some horrific news from back home. John's mum had sadly passed away suddenly at the age of sixty. Total shock set in, the last time we'd seen her was just over a week ago when she was waving us off at the airport. Within forty-eight hours of receiving this news, we had cut the holiday short and had landed back in the UK to be with the rest of John's family.

The next few weeks that followed were difficult. John's mum's funeral took place and everyone was trying to come to terms with her loss.

Chapter 11

After the awful events of the previous few weeks, we all tried to return to some normality. I focused on looking at stallions, it gave me a new purpose. It was clear in my mind the endurance career would be on hold for the foreseeable. This would hopefully give me time to get over my irrational mindset and look forward to a new chapter.

I spent weeks looking at literally hundreds of stallions on the internet. I knew exactly what I was hoping to breed. Breeze, at 14.2 hands, was just about the minimum height for me and with her build, I was possibly right at her weight limit. So, as I was breeding for myself, I would ideally need something around 15 hands with a more solid build than Breeze.

I wanted a stallion with similar colouring to her, bay, black mane and tail – Breeze has three white socks, one black and a white uneven strip down her nose. I wasn't concerned about markings on a stallion though or the colour of its legs. A calm nature was essential in the hope the foal would not inherit Breeze's spookiness.

Eventually I found a stallion which stood out for me a mile above any others. He stood at 15.3 hands and was very similar in colour to Breeze. He was a pure (Asil) Arabian stallion, 100% Bahraini blood. Advanced level in endurance and had successfully competed in show jumping, dressage and ridden Arabian classes. He was much more solid than Breeze and was advertised as having a gentle, kind nature. He was a perfect all-rounder and had proved himself with his offspring too.

I rang the stud farm and asked lots of questions before making my final decision. The stud farm was around a four-hour drive from us so I decided as breeding season was nearing its end, if I was to have Breeze covered this year, I needed to make a decision fairly quickly as to whether I was going to go and see the stallion in person first, or make arrangements for Breeze just to go. Based on all the information, history and photographs I had seen, I was happy to go with the latter.

I contacted the stud farm again and spoke to a lovely lady who made all the arrangements and talked me through how Breeze would be cared for whilst she was there. Before she could go, Breeze had to be tested for Equine Viral Arteritis (EVA) and Contagious Equine Metritis (CEM) which are the required pre-breeding health checks. I made arrangements for the vet to come and carry these out, then with the results back within a few days we were given the all clear to proceed.

The following weekend, we set off on the long drive with Breeze. With a trailer it took much longer than four hours as we took it steady.

When we arrived, we were greeted by the owner of the stud farm and her daughter. They made us feel very welcome. Once Breeze was stabled and settled, we were given a guided tour. I was perfectly happy Breeze was being left in very capable hands and would be well looked after but it was hard for me to leave her as she was such a long way from home and I had no idea how long she would be away. It could be a month if the first covering went well or it could be two or three.

We were taken to see the stallion we had chosen and he was brought onto the yard for us to see how he moved. He was even more stunning in real life and exactly how I'd pictured him. A real gentleman. We were shown all the other stallions and their yearlings which had been bred by the stud. We also saw the mares owned by the stud and visiting mares. The whole set-up was impressive and also the way it was operated. After a lengthy conversation about Breeze's routine and what the plan was for covering, we left and began the long drive back home.

It was strange being home without her to look after. We still had our beautiful Shetland companion pony at home, but she was out at grass and seemed quite happy to have the full paddocks all to herself. She called out during the first few days Breeze wasn't there but other than that she was fine.

I was kept up to date with how Breeze was doing and within two weeks, the phone call came to say she was in season and would be covered the next day. We would then have to wait fifteen days before she could be scanned to see if she was in foal.

It was an agonizing wait. We would be on holiday abroad by then. I remember it clearly. I was sunbathing on the beach and constantly checking my phone to see if I'd missed a call! Eventually by late afternoon, the call came.

'Congratulations, Breeze is in foal.'

I was over the moon and could not wait to get home from holiday so we could go and bring her home.

We came back from holiday and the next day attached the trailer to the car and began the long journey to go and collect her.

We arrived mid-morning. Breeze was out in the field. I had this vision of how she would see me, whinny and run over to greet me. She did none of these and just carried on grazing.

I went into the field, put her headcollar on and gave her a carrot then led her to our trailer. She refused to load! She had stallions calling out to her from across the field. She had obviously been very happy there. Eventually we were on our way on the long journey back.

From this day onwards she would be wrapped in cotton wool until the baby was born!

The next eleven months went by quickly and without any issues as Breeze became enormous, waddling down the field each day for her feed.

During these months, I had been going to the local riding school and joining in the group lesson in the hope at getting my confidence back. With hindsight it didn't really help. All of the horses going around the sand paddock were just like sheep following each other and were very set in their routine. I didn't feel like I was controlling a horse, more like I was just sitting there holding the reins waiting for the horse to follow the one in front. At least I was back in the saddle. Riding round a manège offers a level of security unlike riding in a large open space.

We were three weeks away from Breeze's due date and I was sitting in our garden watching her grazing. She seemed a little unsettled so I decided to stable her and keep a close watch. Her stable was full of bales of deep straw, ready for foaling.

Revisiting this next part of my story breaks my heart all over again, bringing a lump to my throat and tears to my eyes. It's very difficult for me to put down on paper as it forces me to relive the horrific events which followed that night...

Droplets of milk were now coming fast from Breeze's teats so it was obvious foaling would be imminent. It was early evening as myself and John watched from outside the stable. Breeze was restless so we were expecting to see a foal within half an hour. Our sons came down to the stables to watch from a distance. They were fifteen and thirteen years of age at the time. It soon became clear things were not going well and we needed the vet quickly. I sent the boys back into the house.

It was an agonising wait for the vet and we could do nothing more than watch Breeze, who was clearly distressed and in pain. The vet greeted me on our driveway as I directed her to the stable. I was panicking as she tried to console me.

'Don't worry, we'll have baby out in a minute, both of them will be fine,' she said, trying to comfort me.

She examined Breeze and the mood in the stable changed immediately as she announced, 'The foal is dead and we need to get it out quickly before we lose the mare too.'

John went into the stable to try to help as Breeze lay on the stable floor making noises I have never heard before and never want to hear again.

I just sank to my knees on the yard in total shock and broke down. I had never prayed in my life but found myself praying to God, 'You've taken our beautiful foal – please don't take my mare too.'

The vet was struggling, the foal was too big for her to turn round and was stuck. She phoned her practice for help – a colleague who was a cattle vet. He had a long way to travel to get to us and by now it was the early hours of the morning and becoming light. Another agonising hour passed. I was just numb.

I was needed in the stable, but I didn't want to go in. I couldn't watch but had to sit on the floor next to Breeze's head to try and keep her still whilst John and the vet were still struggling to get the foal out. I was talking to Breeze with tears rolling down my face. In the blur of all this a syringe appeared with the vet warning me I was facing a strong possibility of my beautiful Breeze being euthanised – then the second vet arrived. He was bigger and stronger and in a few minutes the foal – a beautiful bay filly – had been delivered – dead. Until this point, I was hoping and praying she would be alive but this was not to be.

With the beautiful filly now lying dead in the deep straw at the back of the stable, I remember both vets working on Breeze as I, in a daze, left the stable. I remember looking around seeing blood splattered all over the walls and the straw.

By some miracle, Breeze was hanging in there fighting for her life.

Both vets came out of the stable looking exhausted and said the next few hours were critical. Breeze was heavily sedated and pumped full of painkillers. We all stood on the yard in silence. I was advised to shut her top door and leave her for a couple of hours to rest and try to get some rest ourselves. Arrangements were made for the vet to return in a couple of hours too.

We closed the stable door and went into the house. Both my husband and I were absolutely drained. We climbed into bed but I could do nothing more than sob my heart out. I was devastated, we both were. Our boys were expecting to see a beautiful foal when they woke up and we were instead delivering terrible news.

Although we were both worn-out we couldn't sleep. I couldn't stop crying. An hour passed then we were up and back down to the stable. I was too scared to open the door in case Breeze was dead. As I slowly opened the top door and peered in, she was at the back of the stable nuzzling her foal. It was heartbreaking to see her. She didn't understand why her baby wasn't acknowledging her.

The vet arrived shortly after and Breeze was given more pain relief then we were faced with the reality of having to take the foal out of the stable away from her.

I couldn't be party to seeing Breeze's beautiful filly removed from her. John and the vet were amazing and shielded me from this. I desperately wanted to go in and stroke her but I couldn't bring myself to do this, something I deeply regret. As I stood at the door glancing towards the back of the stable where the filly was, I could see she had a white marking on her head shaped liked a diamond and was the same colour as Breeze. She was perfect.

The issue of a post-mortem was raised but I refused. Knowing how our foal had died would not have brought her back, I would never send Breeze to stud again so I couldn't learn anything which could help next time. Plus, I blamed myself anyway. I should have called the vet much earlier. This feeling of guilt will never leave me for as long as I live.

Breeze was still extremely poorly and we muddled through each hour of each day round the clock, with frequent vet visits and intensive care at home. Breeze should have been in an equine hospital but she was ill to move. She slowly turned a corner and with some apprehension I dared to believe she would be OK. She was getting stronger each day. On the fifth day, John and I had tickets to a large annual show in Cheshire. Obviously leaving Breeze all day for me was absolutely out of the question. But I was persuaded to take a break and John made arrangements for Breeze to be cared for. Reluctantly, I agreed I would leave her for the morning and just go to the show for a few hours.

As we got in the car and drove off our driveway, it was nice to feel some normality. It was a beautiful sunny day, perfect for the show. I was so tired as I'd been setting my alarm for every two hours during the night to monitor Breeze and not sleeping much in between. I dosed off in the car during what should have been about an hour-long journey. I woke up to find us stuck in the most horrendous traffic jam trying to get into the parking area of the show ground. Within half an hour we had not moved at all and the car started overheating. John managed to pull over onto a grass verge and had to walk to a garden centre near by to see if he could get some water. I sat in the car.

Finally, we parked in the showground parking area and I was already turning my attention to needing to go home. We had already been away for several hours by now and I was panicking. I'd already rang home several times and been told Breeze was fine.

We wandered around the show, watched a bit of show jumping and one of the Arab classes, tasted some cheese in one of the huge tents, had a spot of lunch, then I wanted to go home. We made our way back to the car with John assuring me we wouldn't have any problems with it again going home. Famous last words. Within ten minutes it overheated again and we had to pull over. This time we were miles away from anywhere. I lost my temper with him, shouting, 'I knew this was a mistake, we should never have come.' I wasn't staying with the car on my own, so we both started walking to find somewhere, anywhere, we could get some water from. After what seemed like forever, we stumbled across the little garden centre again where John had got the water from earlier. Armed with water, we set off back on the long walk to the car. I was praying the car would get us home without any more problems. Thankfully, it did, but by the time we got home I was more stressed than ever. Breeze was fine.

As the days turned into weeks and the weeks turned into months, she made a remarkable recovery. She had suffered some internal damage which meant another foal was out of the question. For me, it was out of the question regardless of this after what she'd been through. So that was the end of another chapter.

Chapter 12

I watched Breeze grazing in the paddock as I sat in our garden. Recovery from this for both of us was going to take some time. I was racked with guilt. She would never have had to endure this suffering if it hadn't been for me. I took her to stud; maybe I didn't call the vet quickly enough on that awful night? I didn't do enough otherwise this wouldn't have happened.

I struggled to sleep; every time I shut my eyes the events of that awful night played out in my mind in every little detail. I would wake up in the morning thinking I'd just had the most dreadful nightmare then open my eyes hoping to see Breeze and her beautifully filly out together in the field. Then the cruel harsh reality would set in.

Lightening had struck twice.

When I was twelve years old, my mum and dad bought me a grey Connemara pony, Misty. She arrived one Friday night in May. I dashed home from school to see her. I would ride her every day, I loved her. Nothing fazed her at all and I spent all the school summer holidays with my friends riding around the countryside where we were lucky enough to live.

Around the summertime, Misty was looking well and gaining weight. Julie said she thought Misty could be in foal. We decided to rule this in or out and I remember following Misty around our back garden with an empty jam jar trying to obtain a urine sample. The pregnancy test was negative.

Summer rolled into autumn then a bad winter set in. I went to the farm where Misty was kept near our house. I was in the yard getting Misty's stable ready to bring her in for the night, when one of the girls ran to me screaming; Misty had foaled in the field and the foal was dead.

I ran to the field and the horrific confirmation was staring me in the face. Misty was stood over a dead frozen foal covered in fresh snow. I caught Misty and led her to her stable to wait for the vet. My friend and her mum carried the foal. The vet had said to put the foal in the stable for a couple of days, so Misty could come to terms with her loss.

When the foal was taken away a few days later, Misty went berserk when she was turned out in the field, galloping up and down calling for her baby. It was awful to see.

I had owned her for nine months, so she was actually two months pregnant when she was bought for me and we didn't know. Whether the dealer she came from knew, we would never know.

So here I was again, going through a similar heartbreaking situation.

Breeze had a month in the field before thoughts turned again to starting to exercise her. She was looking well and had her strength back. She is one tough mare!

By now Breeze had not been ridden for well over a year. The last time I had ridden her had not gone well and my mindset riding her had not really changed. Luckily Julie was on hand again and offered to ride her. Breeze stood quite happily whilst she was tacked up and she let Julie mount her. Julie rode down the lane as I walked at the side. You would never have known Breeze hadn't been ridden for such a long time and it was easy to see she was loving being back out again.

I had my riding hat with me and a lead rope so there was no excuse for me not to have a ride too. Once we were both happy Breeze was settled, we swopped over. Julie clipped the lead rope onto Breeze's bit and I took the reins and mounted her.

Julie started to lead me down the track.

All I could do was panic. Looking back with hindsight, for no apparent reason, I was shouting I wanted to get off. Breeze wasn't doing anything apart from walking her naturally quick pace, which always felt like she was going to explode beneath me. Julie was trying to reassure me there was nothing to worry about. There was nothing around us which could have spooked Breeze in any way, shape or form. Just us, on a quiet lane. Perfect surroundings for my first ride.

I managed to stay gripped on for a few more paces then announced I was getting off, then I did just that. Julie patiently unclipped the lead rope, passed it to me then gathered Breeze's reins and got back on her. We walked back home. I carried my riding hat, head down, disappointed and annoyed with myself yet again.

Once home and with Breeze settled, I went into the kitchen, made myself a strong cup of tea and sat with my head in my hands, totally fed up.

Was this how it was going to be from now on? I'd got this beautiful horse with a great endurance career ahead of her – I knew as I'd already started the journey. I knew she could do it and I knew I could do it – but it would appear now – I couldn't. I'd lost all rational belief in myself and I found myself too afraid to even attempt to take Breeze out for a ride, something I'd done lots of times before with no issue or anxiety.

I was back to relying on my husband leading me around again. I would try to use the dog as an excuse. 'The dog needs a walk, so why don't I ride Breeze at the same time?' Sadly, though, we ended up in exactly the same place we had before the foal, it was causing arguments and the issue of selling her was raised again. As far as I was concerned this was not an option, I would never sell her.

Julie kept coming over and riding Breeze and I could see every time how well-behaved Breeze was and all the issues I had, or thought I had, were just in my head.

Chapter 13

So, as it was clear riding Breeze was beginning to look like a thing of the past, so I thought I'd see if I could find a horse to loan. By pure coincidence, Julie had a friend with a horse she felt would be perfect for me. She was a Connemara/Irish draft, around 14.2 hands and sixteen years old. Julie put me in touch with Maureen, the owner, and we had a long chat.

To be honest, I wrote down on a piece of paper exactly what I needed from a horse and it seemed so far-fetched, I thought it was impossible or I was looking for the same as hundreds of other people, so I absolutely struck gold when 'Tilly' came into my life.

I arranged to go and take Tilly out for a ride, with a view to loaning her. My husband was relieved I wasn't looking to buy as he envisaged two horses stuck in the field without a rider! Julie was also concerned about the possibility of me having two I wouldn't ride and didn't want that on her conscience either, being the one who had recommended Tilly!

John took me over to Maureen's to meet Tilly. A grey mare was stood on the yard, tacked up and ready to go. I didn't think for one minute Tilly would be grey! Not a colour I would ever have considered again as they always seemed mucky and notoriously difficult to keep clean! However, if this mare ticked all my other necessary boxes, then I wouldn't have cared if she had been yellow with pink spots on!

Maureen had her other horse tacked up ready so we could ride together but I was too nervous and wanted to see her ride Tilly, especially as the first turning out of the yard was a really busy main road in the centre of a town. I had visions of this horse spooking at a car and jumping into the path of another so I didn't want to be the one on board in case this happened. I didn't plan on blindly getting on a horse I hadn't seen ridden.

Maureen quickly untacked her other horse and turned her out in the field, then we turned our attention to taking Tilly out together. We set off out of the yard, Maureen on Tilly, with me walking alongside. We left the yard and headed towards the busy main road. I was watching Tilly's reaction as a huge wagon thundered past us – she did not bat an eyelid! A second, third, fourth wagon, loads of fast noisy cars, motor bikes, a tractor etc., again no reaction whatsoever. I knew I was looking at a very special mare. We crossed the road and carried on for a mile or so towards the local park.

At this point, I felt confident enough to ride. Maureen dismounted, adjusted the stirrups for me then I mounted. Even though Tilly was the same height as Breeze, she felt so much bigger due to her breed. I instantly felt safe on her. She was solid and it felt like sitting on a big comfy armchair. I always felt like I was just perched on Breeze!

I trotted Tilly around the edge of the park, along the road then back towards the yard. She felt fantastic and I knew she and I could be great together. I felt totally in control. I arranged to go back a few days later and this time, go for a hack-out with Maureen and both horses. I was really looking forward to it and went home feeling positive about riding again. John was pleased we'd found a beautiful horse for me to have some fun with and hopefully get out endurance riding again. When we got home, I was so excited, I rang Julie to fill her in on my day.

On the second ride, Maureen and I went together. It was fantastic. We crossed busy roads, were passed by lorries, cars and motor bikes, we rode through a park full of children playing football, dogs running around, parents pushing prams and again, Tilly was not fazed by anything. We had a great canter up a long track, lots of trotting and I felt 100% safe on her.

The following weekend, Maureen suggested bringing Tilly to my house and leave her for the day. This was a great idea as I would ride her and see what Breeze and Janey (my Shetland pony) thought of her. Breeze was chief mare and I needed to be sure any horse I brought into the mix fitted in and did not change the dynamics we had already established.

As Maureen pulled up our driveway with Tilly in the trailer, Breeze and Janey ran down the paddock calling out. Tilly called back. Once unloaded I put Tilly in one of the stables and put her tack in my tack room. Maureen left and we agreed she would come back around tea time, so I had Tilly for a full day.

I planned to take Tilly on one of my favourite hacks around the local reservoirs. John was going to walk the dog alongside me, our beautiful Labrador Ellie. This time though, we wouldn't be taking a lead rope and I wouldn't be jumping off panicking. The ride was a great success. We were out a couple of hours and when we returned to the yard, I put Tilly in the stable to take her tack off then turned her out in the paddock next to Breeze and Janey so they could meet over the fence. I didn't want bossy Breeze chasing Tilly.

I had no worries at all. Although Tilly was bigger and stronger, she got on great with the others and obviously didn't give off any body language to suggest she was looking at taking chief mare position. The day had been a huge success! John was pleased too, it looked like he could finally get his life back, away from horses! Maureen came back to collect Tilly at the end of the day but then announced she was actually looking to sell not loan.

This was going to be a huge decision for me. Loaning was an ideal scenario because if it didn't work out, at least I could hand the horse back. At present, I hadn't encountered any issues with Tilly which could throw a spanner in the works. It was a gamble to buy another horse and potentially have two I didn't ride.

I mulled it over that evening and then decided to broach the subject with John. He had previously said, 'Yes, a loan but don't buy a second horse.' But his reaction totally took me by surprise! 'Yes, buy her.' He could see what an absolute star Tilly was and I don't believe we could have been lucky enough to find another like her. With the decision made I phoned Maureen to give her the news, we agreed a price and arranged to collect Tilly at the weekend.

It's funny but John still maintains all these years later that I apparently agreed to sell Breeze if I bought Tilly, that conversation absolutely never happened and Breeze was most definitely not going anywhere!

Chapter 14

So, after five years of owning Breeze, I was going to be starting a new chapter with Tilly. This made me reflect on where it had all begun for me as a five-year-old.

My grandfather Albert was one of the kindest most genuine people you could ever wish to meet. He was a hard-working family man who had done well in business and he had a passion for horses.

We were lucky enough to live near him and my grandmother and used to visit them regularly. It was in fact on one of these visits that he took me to the local riding stables. In those days, you paid your fifty pence and took the pony out yourself. He would lift me up onto the pony and lead me down the lane. I would just sit holding onto the saddle. We would do this most Sundays then I would have my lunch at their house. My grandmother was a great cook and I always remember that pudding would be something with thick sweet custard you could stand a spoon up in!

As the months went by and I became more confident, my grandfather bought me a riding hat and crop. We continued our visits to the riding stables and I was less reliant on him to lead me. He taught me how to ride. He promised to buy me my own pony for my eighth birthday and said he and I would look after it together. I was so excited.

Nine months before my eighth birthday, tragedy struck. My grandparents were out at a dinner dance when my grandfather suffered a massive heart attack and passed away that night, totally out of the blue. He was only in his fifties. His death left a huge hole in our lives. As I went through my life, I often wondered what our adventures together would have been like, with or without horses. He was a true inspiration and I will never forget him.

I continued to ride but not as often. I mithered my parents for a pony but they didn't know the first thing about caring for one, and to be fair had no interest or time. At the primary school I attended, one of my teachers lived on a farm and she had horses. One of my friends bought a horse from her and it was on a visit to the farm when I saw 'Pal'. He was a little palomino pony who was only three years old and I desperately wanted him. He was adorable. By now I was nearly eleven and had been helping out at the stables, reading lots of books and convinced my parents I would be able to look after him. They finally agreed and so Pal came into my life.

Well, what can I say about Pal? He was the cutest pony I'd ever seen but he was a little sod. I would go to the field and put his headcollar on, no problem, then lead him down the lane to our house. He would make a beeline for the garden, stick his head down and start munching grass and I could never manage to get his head up and would have to go to 'Auntie Sandra' next door but one for help! She was brilliant with him and would come out of her house, lift his head up and get him off the grass for me!

The following year, we bought a bridle and got him used to a bit. I would sit on his back whilst he was distracted eating his tea at first. This progressed to riding him to and from the field. He was ready to do more with now and I needed some help. A friend of my mum's told us about a friend of hers who visited every Wednesday and who had a daughter who was interested in horses and suggested she might like to come up and meet myself and Pal. Hence, I met Julie.

Every Wednesday Julie would come to my house and we would take Pal out. I would ride and Julie walked beside me. We took him on roads to get him used to traffic, which back in the seventies were nowhere near as busy as they are today. We would walk for miles with him and discovered some great places to hack. Sadly, I outgrew him fairly quickly and made the decision to sell him and look for a bigger pony.

Then along came Misty. She was a grey Connemara, formerly named Katie. She came from a local dealer. My mum and I went along to see her after spotting an advert in the local newspaper. We went to view her with one of our neighbours who was also looking for a pony for his daughter at the same time. I vaguely remember there being several horses and ponies at this yard and the owner desperately trying to sell my friend a one-eyed horse.

Anyway, the deal was that Misty would be transported to us on the Friday night along with a second-hand saddle. I didn't even try her out! How times have changed. They would take Pal in part-exchange. I am horrified writing this. I can't believe I let him go to the place Misty came from but I was not yet thirteen years old and I suppose I was excited to be getting a new pony and knew Pal would also get a new home. However, there was a twist to the story and a very happy ending for Pal, when I saw an article in a newspaper of a girl winning a rosette for jumping at a local show – I recognised the pony instantly and the rider was a girl from my school who was also in my year. Of all the coincidences – she had bought him from the dealer and kept him just a few miles away from where I lived, so I was able to go and see him.

Back to Misty. After the foal tragedy, we had to move on and thankfully after a stressful few months, she was OK so we tried to put this behind us, although it was never forgotten. She was a great mare! By now, Julie had bought a beautiful mare and kept her at the same yard where I stabled Misty. We used to ride for hours. One of my favourite things to do was to pass through a little village with a sweet shop. We would dismount outside the shop and whilst I held the ponies, Julie would go in and buy us both a quarter of sherbet and a lolly and we would sit on the wall dipping the lolly into the sherbet! Both ponies stood quietly, they were very obliging. On hot summer days, we would continue our ride well into the open countryside and make a second stop at a beautiful pub in the middle of nowhere. Julie was old enough to go in and buy us both an orange juice. They were great days full of happy memories.

A couple of years passed. Julie moved to another yard, I outgrew Misty, went to college and my passion for horses was put to one side for now. Eventually Misty was sold and that was the end of the chapter. It was always my intention to buy another horse one day, though I didn't think it would be twenty-five years later!

Chapter 15

So, after a trip down memory lane, here we are collecting Tilly. We went early Saturday morning and as we drove into the yard, there she was ready and waiting for us. She looked great, bathed and spotlessly clean. I was so excited and couldn't wait to take her home. All week I had been worried Maureen might ring me up and say she had changed her mind, as I had done with Breeze a few years ago.

I had hung up a large fresh hay net in the trailer for her, and Tilly just walked straight in and started munching on it. She was not fazed at all. She would walk into any trailer or lorry anytime as I would later discover. Unlike Breeze. I can't say I blame her really. We had an unfortunate incident when John pulled out of a junction too quickly and it clearly scared Breeze. We heard a large clunk in the back of the trailer so guessed she'd lost her footing and knocked herself quite hard. From that day forward it would literally take us anywhere from an hour to two hours to load her, or on a bad day, she wouldn't load at all.

With Tilly secure in the trailer, we started our short journey home. As we pulled up our driveway Breeze called out as soon as she saw the trailer. Tilly called back. I decided to put Tilly in the paddock next to Breeze and Janey as I'd done before so they could get used to each other. It was funny watching them. When Janey went towards the fence, Breeze would chase her away, protecting her. It didn't take long though for them all to settle and within days they were all together. This was a huge relief for me.

After a couple of days, I took Tilly out for a hack. She was incredible. I keep using the phrase 'not fazed by anything', but she literally wasn't. I was so lucky to have her. Don't get me wrong, she wasn't a novice ride because she was so strong and could be awkward but she was bombproof in traffic, happy to be in front or behind, would hack out alone or in company, great to load, shoe, have her teeth done and stand quietly for the vet etc. I couldn't have asked for anything more. She was perfect.

At the end of the month there was a ten-mile charity pleasure ride Julie and Bill were going to and they suggested that I should go along with them and take Tilly. I was definitely up for giving this a go as I'd been hacking out successfully for a few weeks and felt confident enough.

The ride was about an hour away towing the trailer, and as usual Tilly loaded first time no problem and we set off.

At the venue it was busy with lots of horses and riders about. By the nature of this ride, we were going to be passing horses and horses were going to be passing us. Maureen had done years of endurance events on Tilly so she knew the ropes and what was expected of her.

We parked up and unloaded Tilly. John held her whilst she grazed and I went to the Secretary's tent to register and collect my numbered bib. Then I went to find Julie and Bill. They had a horse box so would be parked on a hard standing area.

Now it was time to tack up and start the ride. As this was not a competitive ride, there wasn't any vetting or farrier at this event, so once we were mounted, we were off.

We set off along a flat field next to a stream, I rode in front with Julie behind me, then Bill behind Julie. A number of horses were headed out at the same time so our horses were really excited. Tilly began bunny hopping as I struggled to keep her walking. At first, I was thinking, *What am I doing?* And I started to panic a little, with flashbacks from my last ride on Breeze.

We entered a gate area which led to a big open uphill field. It was pretty chaotic with too many horses around the gate and some horses getting quite giddy and backing into others. Thankfully none of this barging bothered Tilly. On the other hand, if any horse had got too close to Breeze or backed into her, it would have felt the full force of her hind legs. She was always ridden at any event with the compulsory red ribbon in her tail which warns other riders to keep well away.

With the gate cleared we headed up the field. As Tilly started trotting to try and catch up with the horses in front, I could feel myself getting anxious but Bill shouted words of encouragement from behind. At that point Tilly was trying to break into a canter and I could hear Bill say, 'Let her go.' So, I did! And it was fantastic! The three of us cantered along with me leading. We approached many horses along the way with us slowing down and asking permission to pass before we would set off cantering again.

This was a ten-mile ride and was over in a flash. I'd loved it so much I was gutted when we saw the venue ahead, and as I headed back to my trailer and dismounted, I had a huge smile on my face and couldn't stop beaming. I'd never thought this day would come. We had cantered and trotted most of the way on the grass tracks and none of our three horses had even broken a sweat, they were all so fit.

With the horses given half an hour to wind down and graze, we put the tack away and bought ourselves a cold drink and a bacon butty. A great way to end the day before we proceeded to load the horses and go our separate ways home.

This was pretty much the last ride of the season but it was my intention to pursue an endurance career with Tilly the following year and I was excited to see where this would lead us on a new adventure together!

I had a huge smile on my face all the way home, so did John! Tilly was an absolute superstar.

Chapter 16

It was a pretty uneventful winter. Julie came over on a regular basis to ride, weather permitting, and we would hack both Tilly and Breeze out together. I hadn't ridden Breeze in ages. I didn't feel I needed to as she was getting exercised anyway and I had Tilly to ride. I would take Tilly out on her own in between Julie's visits and found my passion for riding again.

It was soon coming around to the start of the endurance riding season and we had managed to maintain both horses' fitness levels so it was only a case of stepping up the speed now and length of time spent in the saddle.

It was early spring and I decided to take Tilly to a pleasure ride and join her previous owner, Maureen. Maureen and I had kept in touch after I bought Tilly and had become good friends. This ride was one I had done years ago on Breeze which I had completely forgotten about! It was at a place called Shipley Park.

As we left the house with Tilly in the trailer, it was a cold March morning and there was ice and frost on the ground. I did wonder if we were making a mistake. Conditions were not good for riding. As it was only 7am, I hoped by the time we reached the venue, the temperature might have risen a couple of degrees, enough to thaw the ice. It was going to be a couple of hours yet before we would arrive and be ready to ride, so it was plausible.

We joined the motorway and stuck to the inside lane, taking it slowly. We had been travelling for less than an hour, when suddenly, it was as if someone had attached a bungy line to the back of the car and pulled us backwards. There was nobody else around. Shocked and baffled, we pulled over onto the hard shoulder to check the car and trailer. Both John and I got out and looked around.

Everything was fine on the outside. I opened the jockey door to check on Tilly. She was stood eating hay with her thick leather headcollar snapped and hanging off her head. The lead rope she was tethered with was wrapped around her hay net. It soon became clear she had pulled back, probably because her rope had got stuck and the force had snapped her headcollar and pulled the car back. I knew she was strong as I'd witnessed her bend a thick steel bolt back when she once barged out of her stable. Quite frightening really.

I had to try to repair the headcollar with baling twine to secure it and we set off on our way. Thankfully, the rest of the journey was fine and we arrived at the venue a little while later. The ground conditions hadn't improved nor had the temperature risen any. It was freezing. With Tilly out of the trailer and tacked up, Maureen and I were ready to set off. Even though I had two jumpers on, a thick coat, gloves, two pairs of socks and riding boots, I was still freezing cold.

There were many different routes in the park to choose from which meant we had horses coming past us in different directions. We picked a route to follow and I tried to settle a very excited Tilly. She was so strong I was struggling to keep my seat and keep contact with her. As we turned onto an icy track, we saw a number of horses ahead of us and that was it, Tilly decided she was catching them up. She bunny hopped sideways and picked up speed. I was trying desperately to calm her down, all to no avail. Suddenly she was gone. I was hanging on with everything I had as she was sliding on the ice and careering down the track at a flat-out gallop. The horses ahead went around the corner out of sight so Tilly went faster. I was stood up in my stirrups pulling back with all my might but I could not stop her. Ahead on the track, I could see some walkers and one of them was pushing a trolley with a toddler in it, I knew Tilly wouldn't stop, she would just plough straight through them so I screamed at the top of my voice for them to get out of the way.

This was the first time I was also wearing my new air jacket. In my head I believed that day it wouldn't be a question of 'if' it would activate but 'when', as I was sure I would be on the ground any minute. The air jacket was attached to my saddle by a lanyard and if the lanyard became detached following a fall, then the air jacket would inflate instantly. I'd had a demonstration in the shop when I bought it and it was an amazing piece of safety kit.

By some miracle, I was still hanging on when we approached the next corner and Tilly slowed down as she was running out of breath and the horses ahead were no longer in sight. I managed to bring her under control, unclipped my lanyard and jumped off her immediately. That was it. I didn't want to get back on, I couldn't get back on, she was spinning around me and rearing up and I could barely hold her. We were both sliding all over the track on the ice.

A guy who was walking along offered to help, which was welcomed. Maureen asked me if I wanted her to get on Tilly. I was grateful for that but I said I'd lead her horse. If Tilly went off again, I'd be following on a horse I had never ridden and that wasn't something I was happy to trial today. My legs were still like jelly. Between this guy and myself, we managed to hold Tilly long enough for Maureen to mount and we tried to walk for a while. We came to an area where it was safe for us to swap over and I got back on her. After a few minutes we were caught up again by another group of horses and I decided enough was enough.

There were too many horses around, too many people and it was still cold and icy. Conditions underfoot were still dangerous. I managed to ride back to my trailer and John, who was surprised to see me so soon. I explained what had happened followed by the fact I wanted to go home. It was a long drive back and I remember falling asleep in no time at all. We had been up really early and I was cold and tired. I was woken by the sound of a car horn. I opened my eyes to the horror of my trailer wandering into the overtaking lane as John had shut his eyes for a split second with tiredness. That could have been disastrous. We were very lucky.

As we pulled up the driveway, Breeze and Janey called out to Tilly and Tilly called back. I led Tilly back to her stable and fed all three of them before turning them all out for the remaining few hours of the day. I unloaded the trailer, put all the tack away and went into the house to thaw out. John made us a welcome cup of tea then I fell asleep on the chair absolutely exhausted.

Chapter 17

I woke up the next morning feeling really disappointed with myself. We went all that way for me to literally be in the saddle for about half an hour. On reflection, I should have gone back to the trailer and given Tilly time to calm down, or waited until there were fewer riders out on the trail, then gone back out on her instead of trying to get away from the venue as soon as possible.

I had my breakfast then wandered down to the stables. Breeze whinnied as always which was lovely to hear. They all waited patiently for their feeds and hay nets, then whilst they all had their heads in their buckets, I skipped out and gave them all fresh water. They all had automatic water feeders in their stables, but chose not to use them. Breeze especially didn't like the sound of it refilling. I left them munching on hay and went back up to the house. It was a pleasant morning but cold. I decided to give Tilly an hour or so to let her breakfast settle then I would ride her. I had to ride her that day.

I put her bridle and saddle on and as I mounted her, surprisingly, I didn't feel any anxiety at all and had a lovely hack-out. We passed a few tractors and a couple of people with a loose dog running around. I had a lovely trot down the lane and all the fear from yesterday had already gone. I cantered up to my usual spot and just let her go then made my way back home. So, once sat back in my kitchen, I made myself a cup of tea and had a look at the Endurance GB schedule to decide what my next ride could be. I phoned Julie to ask her opinion. Following a long discussion, we came to the conclusion that Wharncliffe Chase would be suitable. It wasn't too far away and Julie had ridden it on many occasions so knew the course. We both sent off our entries. I was nervous about this; I have to admit. So far, I had had one absolutely fantastic ride on Tilly and one complete disaster, so it was impossible to judge how the next one would go.

This ride was in June so we had plenty of time to bring fitness levels up ready for the twenty miles we would be riding. I went on holiday at the end of May and would be back two days before the ride.

For most of my holiday, the ride was playing on my mind as it was getting closer. But it was just nice to spend a week chilling on the beach and swimming in the beautiful clear sea. As the holiday came to an end, we arrived home to news that Tilly was lame. It was quite apparent she would not be sound within the next few days and it was sadly confirmed by the vet. Following a series of ultrasounds and X-rays, it appeared she had damaged her check ligament

If I was reading this story, I would swear it was fiction as I would find it hard to believe anyone could have such bad luck. I kid you not, this is all the truth.

This lameness resulted in me receiving the news that Tilly needed box rest, and twelve weeks of it. Three whole months with no turnout. Not only did it have consequences for Tilly but also for Breeze and Janey. So, to avoid Tilly getting stressed seeing them go out and possibly making the damage to her ligament even worse, the other two stayed in at night near her. The beauty of our own place meant we could create a small grazing area near Tilly so she could see the others during the day. I soon got into a routine and the time passed fairly quickly. Tilly had been a perfect patient. Her only vice was trying to barge out of the stable once the door was opened. She had no regard whatsoever for anyone's personal space. If you were in her way, she would mow you down. Thankfully the solution to this was to keep the door fastened back open at all times and substitute it with just a thin chain clipped across. Worked a treat. She never once tried to get under or over it and it obviously cured the panic she felt at having the door closed on her, even though it was just the bottom half.

During her box rest, I was cold-hosing her legs twice a day, she would wear magnetic boots at night and she had regular physiotherapy. At the end of the twelve weeks, our vet confirmed she was sound enough to start turning out. At this point only light exercise was permitted and small paddock turnout, so it meant the competitive riding season for us was over before it had begun. Yet more disappointment.

Even more bad news was to follow, before the end of autumn she came trotting towards the field gate one evening, clearly lame on the other front leg and once again it was confirmed she had damage to that check ligament. We ended up back at square one following the same procedure as before with the box rest etc. If there was any justice, the vet said it wasn't uncommon for this to happen and at least it had happened in the same season. We had a good chance of Tilly making a full recovery for the following year.

So, with Tilly out of action, I turned my attention to Breeze. I did intend to ride her locally but Julie was happy to ride her on occasion competitively. I was delighted with this as Breeze, as we already knew, was ideal for endurance, but there was a hurdle we would have to get over first: the loading issue.

A few years ago, Julie and I went to a demonstration of a well-known trainer in natural horsemanship. Or in modern terms, a 'horse whisperer'. One of the sections included loading a stubborn horse, which he did, without any issues at all. So, I made enquiries and enlisted the help of one of his associates. I am always very sceptical about these things and my belief in this type of horsemanship would only be if I saw Breeze, with my own eyes, loaded by a stranger using these methods.

A couple of days later this great character arrived. I was asked to move my trailer into an open space, open the front and back ramps and remove the partition. This gave a great area to work with. He put a dually headcollar on Breeze and proceeded to 'join up' with her by leading her into and around my sand paddock. There he began by rubbing her face and having her following him around. Every now and again he would stop, push her back a few paces then let her walk on with him. When he stopped, she stopped. When he went forward, she went forward. Then he took her headcollar off and did exactly the same. She followed him everywhere and whenever he stopped, she stopped directly behind him, never once attempting to pass him. He then walked towards and trailer and jogged up the ramp. 'This will be fun,' I thought. 'This is where it all goes pear-shaped.' But no, I swear on my life, she followed him straight up the ramp and through the trailer. Not just once either but repeatedly. She still didn't have a headcollar on!

Watching his relationship with her in minutes was just unbelievable. He'd managed to do what I still hadn't in years. He wanted to see how she reacted with me, so he put the headcollar back on her and passed me the lead rope and asked me to take her into the sand paddock and lead her up and down. As I did this, he observed. Breeze did her usual, get ahead of me whilst I tried to keep up. Interestingly, he said that from our partnership, she was the one in charge, not me. It made perfect sense to be honest.

Within the hour, I was taught about 'schooling' her with a headcollar, which was all about pressure release. When she didn't walk where I was asking her to, I pulled on the headcollar which in turn put pressure on her nose. When she did as I asked, I released the pressure which was the reward. She is a very clever mare so she soon got the hang of it.

Then it was my turn to load her. Using the skills I had just been shown, I walked towards the trailer with Breeze behind me on a short lead rein. As I stepped onto the ramp,

I expected the rope to suddenly tighten in my hand as it had many times before when she would stop dead and refuse to budge. Not this time – I kept looking ahead and the rope still loose in my hand as I walked into the trailer, she was right with me! We did the same process time and time again!

The following day I practised with the pressure release headcollar and loaded her several times. *Surely it can't be this easy?* I thought. Delighted with the results, I felt now, with some confidence, that I would be able to take her to a competitive ride with Julie.

Chapter 18

Now the plan was to increase both Tilly and Breeze's fitness. With Tilly recovered from lameness we rode both over the winter and into spring. We hoped to take them both to Wharncliffe Chase. The only issue we had now was that Breeze was used to loading in a trailer without the partition. I had bought two double breast bars for safety and travelling her in this way was working, so Tilly would be travelling to the venue in Julie's horse box.

Deja vu, here we were again! It was May and John and I had gone away on holiday for a week and the ride would be a few days after we got back home. I couldn't believe a whole year had passed by already.

We arrived home to find two sound horses so we would definitely be riding Wharncliffe Chase that year. I had not taken Tilly to a ride since the disaster at Shipley Park so was apprehensive to say the least. The plan was that Julie would ride lead on Breeze and I would tuck Tilly close behind her. I was pinning my hopes on riding her right behind Breeze and hoping the pecking order we had at home would continue when the adrenaline rush kicked in and she would not try to pass Breeze and take off no matter what anybody else's horses were doing.

The day of the ride arrived. I had prepared for it the night before and loaded the majority of the items I needed for both horses already as I knew my head would be all over the place in the morning. I didn't get much sleep either. All possible scenarios were racing through my mind.

Julie and Bill arrived early with their horse box. I loaded Breeze first in my trailer then once she was secure, I dashed to Tilly's stable. She already had a headcollar on so I attached a lead rope and walked her across the yard to Julie's horse box as quickly as possible. By now Breeze was creating a bit of a commotion in the trailer because it was still stationary. She was whinnying and stamping her front leg hard on the floor. Tilly was whinnying back which didn't help. As we approached the ramp, I didn't know if Tilly would actually walk up it. She'd never been in a horse box before. Thankfully this was no issue at all. She walked straight in and started eating hay. So, with her secure, I dashed back to my trailer and opened the jockey door to check on Breeze to try to calm her down. I knew she'd be fine once we started moving so I jumped into the passenger seat of the car and John slowly set off following the horse box.

It was about an hour's drive but it was early so there was not much traffic on the roads. We had a good run and were one of the first to arrive at the venue.

Horse boxes were directed to park on the hard standing area whilst 4x4s pulling trailers were directed to park on the grass. So unfortunately, as we had one of each, we couldn't park next to each other. This wasn't a problem though. First thing to do was to unload Breeze before she started stamping again. John walked her around whilst she grazed then I went over to the box to bring Tilly over. They were both calling out when they realised that they were both there!

Julie and I went to the Secretary to register and collect our numbered bibs then back to the horses to go to the vetting area. There were two vets at the event so we were able to trot both horses up and down at the same time thankfully before their heart rates were counted beats per minute. If we hadn't have done it this way, there's no doubt in my mind at least one of them would have had a heart rate through the roof if they thought they'd been separated and they could have failed before the ride had started.

Breeze's heart rate was in the forties as usual and Tilly's in the sixties. Tilly's was always notoriously high, even though she was as cool as a cucumber. It could be literally just one beat away from either a 'pass' or a 'fail'.

With the vetting done, we headed to the farrier for a quick foot inspection. Both had been shod recently and with no loose shoes we were good to go.

We tacked up, got ourselves organised then mounted and I geared myself up for what was to come. We waited until there was a gap in horses going out so we wouldn't be too close to any. The last thing I wanted was for my horses to try and catch up with any in front and take off with us. I was pretty sure Breeze wouldn't do this but you never know.

We passed the timekeeper and went out onto the track. The clock had now started ticking so we needed to start motoring. Julie, on Breeze, was in front, with me behind on Tilly. Both horses had red ribbons on their tails to indicate their liability to kick if you got too close. Although Tilly was quite chilled with horses getting close, Breeze was very protective over her so it would be better if both horses were given a wide berth to be on the safe side.

We approached a long narrow tunnel which for me was not good as I'm claustrophobic. Coupled with the echoing sound of the horses' hooves, I felt myself panicking. Not a great start when we'd gone less than a mile. I heard horses coming up behind us, this would be a test. Tilly was already far too excited and I was struggling to hold her. I was desperately trying to keep her right behind Breeze but not close enough to get a kick. The girls coming up behind us asked permission to pass. I think I squealed a feeble 'Yes', as they slowed down. Tilly started bunny hopping sideways and I thought, 'I'm in trouble' so I jumped off and held her reins tightly just behind the bit. The girls passed us and carried on. By now Tilly was fired up and I didn't want to get back on. At that point I was running with her as we still had to maintain a certain speed. Julie was telling me to get on. It was apparent fairly quickly I couldn't run at this pace. I was already knackered. It was a warm day and I had my riding hat on, long riding boots, which were definitely not ideal to run in, a long-sleeved shirt, jacket gloves and a body protector. Suddenly the fact I couldn't run another step made the decision for me. *Get on quickly and get going.* I pulled myself together, stood Tilly next to a wall and used it as a mounting block and jumped on.

We carried on for the next ten or so miles until we saw our crew. By this point we were riding along roads and up hilly areas so I wasn't too concerned. Tilly tired quite easily going uphill so I knew I could handle her. With a quick sip of bottled water for us, horses sloshed and a drink of sugar beet water, we set off again within minutes. We were right on track timewise as long as we kept up this pace. We didn't see many other horses, which was great, and I began to enjoy the ride. As we came off a track onto a busy road, I took the lead. Tilly was always a calming influence in traffic. As we trotted up a very steep narrow incline we approached a sharp blind bend and to my horror, a lorry came thundering round it. It was as much of a shock for him to see us as much as it was a shock for us. There was no way he could safety apply his brakes so he thundered past us downhill. I was scared to look behind me as I knew this would have freaked Breeze out. As I glanced quickly behind my right shoulder, I couldn't see her, I glanced quickly to my left to see her right up Tilly's left side. Julie had been able to use Tilly as a shield, thank God. A few miles more and we were soon on the homeward stretch having looped back onto the initial tunnel track.

By now we'd ridden some twenty-four miles so were down to the last mile. We had enough time in hand purposely to be able to walk into the venue to get the horses heart rates down and begin cooling them off. Unfortunately, my estimation of how exhausted Tilly would be by now was way off, especially when a pleasure rider passed us at speed and she was fired up again. I had no choice but to sit it out, as one of the rules is that you can dismount on course as many times as necessary but you must be in the saddle as you leave and enter the venue. I only had to get through less than a mile and I would have completed the ride. There was no way I was going to let anything stop me this close to the end, no matter how much I was literally hating every minute.

Finally, the view I had been waiting for, the venue was in sight! As we rode in past the timekeeper, we had a quick time check there, then back to the trailer. With a final dismount and a huge sigh of relief, I pulled my body protector, gloves and hat off and drank a bottle of water. We untacked both horses and began sloshing them down before walking them around to cool off and get their heart rates down. We had a thirty-minute window to achieve this and present to the vet.

We had permission again to trot up together, so with Julie running with Breeze and me Tilly, they both passed that test showing no signs of lameness, then it was heart beats per minute. I was holding my breath as we stood in silence awaiting the results. I wasn't concerned about Breeze as I knew hers was always well within the acceptable parameter. What a relief! Both horses had passed, Tilly by a hare's whisker! I would have been devastated if she'd failed after all the effort which had gone into today.

So, all in all it was a successful day and I was quite relieved it was over!

We now faced a challenge – separating both horses to travel home. Breeze wouldn't load with Tilly still in sight so we had to be a bit crafty. Julie led Tilly through my trailer then I followed with Breeze. Once we had Tilly blocking the outward ramp and Breeze in the body of the trailer behind her, John put the bars in front and back to hold Breeze in, then Julie walked Tilly off the ramp and I closed it quickly. Breeze was going berserk. We had to get going now as soon as possible to get Breeze to settle. John started driving very slowly off the field and I walked Tilly back to the hard standing area to Julie's horse box. With Tilly calling out to Breeze and vice versa, Tilly walked up the ramp again, no problem, and with her securely inside we began the drive home.

We pulled up onto our driveway a short time later, unloaded both horses and turned both out in the paddock. They both got down and enjoyed a good roll over and over.

A triumph of a day!

Chapter 19

With a successful competitive ride completed, Breeze moved up to the next level from 'Novice' to 'Open'. Tilly was already in this group. The next step to get to 'Advanced Level' was a forty-mile ride, followed by a fifty-mile one. Breeze was more than capable of this but I wasn't, which meant Tilly wouldn't be advancing any further. I had back trouble which MRI scans had confirmed, and I had already pushed it too far at Wharncliffe Chase. After being in the saddle for three plus hours doing rising trot most of the way, I was in agony during the days that followed. It was difficult for me to stand up straight without pain and I was practically crawling around. I still had three horses to look after, a house to run and work to go to, so had no chance of getting any rest, I just had to get through it, gritting my teeth and taking medication.

There was a ride coming up with the venue being at a racing stable and due to the distance we would have to travel to get to it, it would mean going the day before and the horses would be stabled there overnight. I was very excited about this event. Julie and I had a chat about it and we decided Bill would ride this time with their daughter Alison. Bill would ride his horse, Alison would ride Breeze and Julie, John and myself would crew.

Julie, Bill and Alison would camp overnight at the venue across the way from the stables and they would look after the horses. John and I booked into a beautiful hotel nearby for the night. I think I was looking forward to this more because I wasn't riding! There was a lot to pack this time. Apart from all the usual, we needed to double up on some items like horse rugs, boots and numnahs. We also needed to take two days' worth of feeds and plenty of full hay nets and buckets. There was plenty to pack for us too for our night in a hotel.

It was the day before the ride and we started with a leisurely morning. We loaded Breeze, surprisingly without too much of a to-do, around lunch time. She was slowly slipping back into her awkward ways of not loading first time. She would walk to the ramp, giving you false hope, stand her front two feet on it then flatly refuse to walk any further. Nothing would persuade her to go in. We'd tried buckets of food, lunge lines round her back side, moving her feet, even waving a broom at her! We would just have to wait until she decided she would walk in. This could take anything from a few minutes to an hour. Believe me, this took some patience and everyone who knows me, knows this is something I do not have!

It would take almost three hours to get to the race course, so the plan was to arrive around tea time, let the horses stretch their legs first of all for a while then get them settled in the stable for the night. Breeze and Dancer had been ridden together on many occasions and were quite happy in each other's company.

A field adjacent to the stables had been designated for parking and camping. We drove onto it and parked next to Bill and Julie's horsebox. The field was dry so there was no issues with getting stuck on the grass.

We opened the trailer and let Breeze have a look around before leading her out. Straight away her head went down to graze. Dancer was grazing nearby. We left the horses with John and Bill so Julie and I could go and find the stables allocated to us and get them ready. They were already deeply bedded with straw so we carried our hay nets across, filled our water buckets and prepared the night feeds. Then with both horses settled, John and I unhooked the trailer, got into the car to drive the mile or so to the hotel.

It was a beautiful hotel in a great location. We had booked to eat in the restaurant that evening. We had a glass of wine each with our meal then it was off to bed. We would need to be back at the stables around 7am the next morning and as it was going to be a long day and John would be driving, we couldn't have a late boozy night!

We were up at 6am the following morning and it was a beautiful day. We checked out of the hotel, had to miss breakfast unfortunately as it was too early, then made our way back to the stables. The horses had already had their feed and were tucking into a fresh hay net. Our horses had been given a vetting time of 9.30am so we had time to get our breakfast at the racecourse and lead the horses out to graze and stretch their legs beforehand.

It was soon time to start getting ready. It has to be the rider who takes the horse to the vet and farrier, so once Bill and Alison had collected their numbered bibs, they headed to the designated area. With both horses passed fit to go, it was time to tack up.

The start of the ride was going out down the actual race track! Alison was in front on Breeze and an excited Dancer was bucking all the way with Bill on board. We waited until they had trotted out of sight then went back to our cars to stock up on crewing supplies and headed out to the first crew point.

It was a popular ride with lots of entries and several horses passed before we saw ours in the distance. Breeze was in the lead with her ears forward and trotting towards us with her incredible pace. Julie tended to Bill and Dancer and I took care of Alison and Breeze. Both horses were glad to gulp down the sugar beet water and appreciated being sloshed and sponged down, then they were on their way. With lids back on water buckets and slosh bottles, we packed everything back into the cars and made our way to the next crew point.

An hour or so later we repeated the same process then we drove back to the venue to wait. Soon Bill and Alison rode in. This was the halfway stage, so we followed the process as we would do at the end of a ride, untacked, cooled the horses down and waited to present to the vet within thirty minutes. Bill checked the horses' heart rates a couple of times and when they were low enough, he and Alison headed off to the vet.

All good, it was time to tack up again, including clean dry numnahs and boots, then off they went. It was the same course as before and the two twenty-mile loops made up the forty miles. We crewed in the same places. After the second checkpoint with our horses on their way and about five miles left to complete, a guy crewing other horses shouted out to us, 'I think the light bay is lame.' We were busy packing the buckets etc., back into the car and when we looked ahead our horses were out of sight. We drove ahead to catch up with them and observe Breeze. She did look a little lame but as we continued to watch, it was hard to tell if she was or if she may have just stood on a stone. At this point, we drove back to the venue to wait for them to come in.

Once they were back, we tried to keep Breeze moving as she looked like she was stiffening up and we just had to get through the last thirty minutes to get to the vet. We continued to cool both horses down and again Bill monitored their heart rates. Unfortunately, Breeze failed the trot up so failed the vetting. I was absolutely devastated. All that team effort for nothing. I was so disappointed and worried about her. She limped back to the stable and I gave her a feed. We all went for our tea to give the horses a chance to rest before we set off on the long drive back home.

The journey back was horrendous with it soon getting dark and the weather turning. We passed remote areas of the Peak District with the wind and rain howling around the trailer and fog so thick it was hard to see the road directly in front of us. This made the journey much longer. We were both relieved to pull up our driveway and hear Tilly whinny. Breeze called back. As we opened the trailer, Breeze struggled down the ramp. I led her to the stable area. Then by opening the gates in a certain way, it gave her the option of either going into the stable or field, whichever she preferred. We then headed up to the house and decided it was too late to start unpacking all the gear. We were shattered, so after a quick cup of tea, it was off to bed.

Chapter 20

I was up early the next morning and looked out of my bedroom window hoping to see Breeze, Tilly and Janey happily grazing, but there was only Janey in sight. I got dressed and hurried down to the stables. It wasn't unusual for them to be stood in their respective stables. The first stable in the row belonged to Breeze so as I popped my head around to look in, I expected her to be there, but there was no sign of her. Next one along was Janey's, also empty. I walked along to Tilly's at the far end and found them both stood side by side in there. When they saw me, they proceeded to walk forward to come out. Tilly was in front and absolutely fine, but Breeze, oh my God, I was shocked, her hindquarters had completely ceased up and you could see the pain on her face as she struggled to move. I immediately called the vet and arranged a visit.

As I waited for the vet, I pulled four bags of shavings out of the barn and put them down in Breeze's stable, then managed to get her to it and closed the stable door to keep her in. You could see how uncomfortable she was. She made no effort to come out anyway nor did she approach the door.

An hour or so later the vet arrived. I knew there wouldn't be much she could do but at least she could administer pain relief. She also suggested I wrap Breeze's back legs in thick pads held in place with stable bandages. The main thing was she didn't appear to have any lasting damage. Box rest followed for the next few days. By the end of the week, she was more or less back to normal. A little stiff but she was happy to potter around the field. She would rest for the next few weeks anyway after a long competitive ride.

It was July and although there were more competitive rides coming up, I decided not to enter anymore. Neither of my horses could achieve a higher level unless they did at least a forty-mile ride. I didn't feel Breeze was fit enough and as I've already said, my back wasn't up to it. So I thought about turning my attentions elsewhere!

There was a local horse show every August and after looking through the schedule, I decided to enter Breeze in the veteran in hand class and the Arab in hand class for a bit of fun. Even though I wasn't taking it too seriously, both Breeze and myself would be kitted out in the ring in the correct manner, so I took to my regular online favourite equine store and bought Breeze a beautiful in hand bridle, new bit and matching lead rope. For myself, a waist coat, white shirt and jacket. It was exciting having a new focus and something I'd never done before.

The day of the show arrived. Breeze had been bathed and stabled the night before. Although she is bay, she has three white socks so I particularly wanted to keep them spotlessly clean. Breeze was shown as a foal and I believe qualified at county level. I do have a photograph of her in the show ring – so beautiful, but I am biased.

Our first class was 10.30am so I had plenty of time to get her ready. It was only a ten-minute walk up a stony narrow track to approach the showground entrance the back way so as to avoid the busy main road. First job of the morning was to brush the remnants of shavings off Breeze from where she had been lying down, then plait her mane and tail. Even though I say so myself, she looked stunning. I was a little disappointed etiquette dictated she needed to be plaited as she had the most amazing long, flowing black mane and tail, which I was really proud of.

I went back up to the house to get myself ready. I teamed my new items with black jodhpurs, long black riding boots then tied my hair back in a ponytail and put my hat and gloves on. We were ready to go. Suddenly I was really nervous and should have known what was about to come given we were local and 'on her patch'.

Walking up the lane was fine but as we entered the showground, Breeze was strong and I was struggling to hold her. She was neighing at the top of her voice constantly and spinning round me, lifting her front feet off the ground. Whenever I took her away from home, she was always fine in unfamiliar surroundings and with other horses as long as they stayed a few feet away from her. But the same could not be said when she was ridden around our home area. It was as if she was protecting her 'patch'. I would always have to ask riders to give her an extra wide berth as she would quicken her pace, put her ears back, snort and start prancing sideways as they passed, and she was worse if Tilly was with her.

I was hoping she would settle as I walked her round. I took her away from the horse area and towards the trailers. It was about twenty minutes until the class. It didn't make a difference though. I thought about just taking her home but I'd put such a lot of effort into this I didn't want to be defeated so I thought I'd go to the ring and at least go in. Worst case scenario, I would have to take her out.

I entered the ring with eight other horses. She was still neighing and trying to spin around me. I had to put one hand on her chest to try to stop her. She bucked out at the horse behind me as I politely shouted, 'Could you please stay well back?'

The judge could see I had my hands full. The more we all circled around the ring, the more I struggled. Then we were all instructed to stop and asked to do our individual trot up. This I was absolutely now dreading. As it got to my turn, I had to trot uphill, up the show ring. As I set off, Breeze exploded and practically left me behind hanging onto the end of the rope. Bear in mind, she is part trotter by breed, so her trot is at a speed I've seen many horses have to canter at to keep up with her.

As I turned at the top of the ring and trotted back down to the judge, my hair bobble fell out letting my long hair down which then was blowing over my face obscuring my vision, further adding to the drama. Breeze would not stand still for the judge and continued the erratic behaviour as I was directed to take her back to the space in the line of horses.

After everyone had done their trot up, we were all instructed to walk around the ring again as the judge began pulling us out to place us. At one point I was pulled out of the line but because I was unable to pay attention to where I should go, I headed to the wrong end of the line and it looked like I thought I was in first place, not sixth. I was mortified. I knew I wasn't placed first but I just wasn't watching where I should go, I was struggling too much and by now was beyond caring and just wanted to get out of the ring as soon as possible.

As I headed to my correct place in the line, the judge came up the line starting with first place. She got to me and handed me a rosette. She also praised me for the way I'd handled madam and told me not to give up. I thanked her but thought to myself, 'I'm never doing this again!' In fact, my only thought then was to get Breeze back home and pour myself a very large gin and tonic despite the fact it was only lunchtime. I was not intending to go back to the second class I had entered later that afternoon.

As we walked the lap of honour the rope closing off the ring was opened and we all headed out. Breeze reared and I couldn't hold onto her any longer despite my best efforts and she broke free. She galloped away at full speed with everyone trying to get out of her way and people yelling 'loose horse'. There were loads of people panicking and trying to avoid being trampled on. Breeze headed towards the trailer area and eventually stopped and was caught by a guy nearby.

I gratefully made my way over to him and took hold of the lead rein. Breeze was all lathered up and I was completely out of breath. Luckily, we were near the exit which led back onto the lane to make our way home.

Breeze was still very excited and still trying to spin around me and as I was on the lane, she reared up again and fell over into a large patch of nettles. This completely shocked her as she scrambled to her feet and shook. She was covered in stings which I have to say after what she had put me through, I thought served her right.

She dragged me down the narrow lane, whinnying all the way. At one point my feet left the ground. As soon as she spotted our house in the distance, she calmed down instantly. I led her up the driveway and straight to the field and turned her out. She ran to Tilly and Janey whinnying and put her head down and started grazing. To see her now, no one would believe the ordeal she'd just put me through.

I went straight up to the house to change into my jeans and a t-shirt. I took my gloves off to look at my right hand, which by now was turning black. No surprise there considering I'd had a lead rein wrapped tightly around it and the full half-ton weight of Breeze on it for the best part of three hours. I sat down beside my dogs with a large gin and tonic in my hand and thought how lucky we'd been nobody got hurt that day. Breeze's showing days were well and truly over!

Chapter 21

We had a pretty uneventful few months following the show – hacking most weekends and enjoying the fact there wasn't any pressure to go out and do anything anywhere. Winter came around and we still managed to hack in between the cold bad weather. Spring came, then summer.

I sadly lost my beautiful Shetland pony in the July due to laminitis, a struggle I had had with her for a long time. I tried everything with her but it got to the point where keeping her in was awful because she hated being stabled, she didn't like soaked hay and she could no longer go out in a grazing muzzle because her feet were too sore. In the end I had to admit defeat and, on the vet's advice, I reluctantly had to have her put down. I was so grateful to Julie. It was she who agreed to come to my house and deal with this difficult and upsetting situation. I just couldn't do it. I waited in the house until Janey had been taken away then I got in my car and drove to the moors. I took myself off for a long run and bawled my eyes out. Janey had been a rescue pony. I could only console myself with the knowledge I had given her a good home for all the years she had been with me. You could see both Breeze and Tilly were affected by her loss as the three of them had been a close-knit little trio.

But life goes on and as we came to terms with our loss, I carried on with my usual daily routine of going down to the stables every morning around 9am. If the horses were out, they would immediately run down, in their pecking order, with Breeze first, Tilly behind and they would go straight into their own stables to wait for their breakfast.

On this particular morning, I caught sight of them heading down whilst I was mixing their feeds. As I turned around, they were still near the top of the paddock which was strange. Breeze was struggling. I watched in horror wondering what an earth she could have done. My first thought was she might have pulled something whilst careering round the field. I watched her slowly make her way down, grimacing. She went into the stable and stood at the back leaning on her hind legs. Instantly I knew she had laminitis. I knew the signs only too well.

What I couldn't understand was how quickly she'd gone downhill from being fine the night before. Well, she wouldn't be going out for a while now so I deep-bedded her in with my emergency supply of shavings and she immediately lay down. I felt so sorry for her, she looked lost lying there. I took the large hay net down and split it across two hay nets, found a large plastic container and filled it with water, dunking the two nets and leaving in the water to soak for at least six hours. I had to call the vet to come out to make Breeze comfortable. Unfortunately for Tilly, this would mean she would be on a different routine for as long as Breeze was on box rest. Luckily, she was really easy going and quite happy to go with the flow.

Poor Breeze was now having to have small soaked hay nets four times a day. She hated soaked hay. Each time I hung a net up, she would spin it around with her nose and pull a face. Then she would step away from it and leave it, only to return to pull out a mouthful and realise if she was hungry then it was this or nothing. She spent the majority of these days lying down. I knew this was going to be a long road to recovery and it would mean her routine would permanently change. I called our farrier out to remove her shoes and he cut her feet back really short. In her front feet there were thin lines of blood, classic laminitis signs.

Breeze was not able to leave the stable for weeks. Towards the end of the third week, she was standing more than lying down and she was moving a little more around the stable. I started turning her out in the sand paddock, building the time up each passing day. The soft sand under her feet was fine and it gave her a chance to stretch her legs and have a roll without any grass whilst I observed.

Before long, she was well enough to go out to grass, but this would be my next challenge. She would have to be muzzled.

The first morning it took ages attaching the muzzle to the headcollar which was specially designed for it. Then fitting it correctly on Breeze, making adjustments to ensure it was not too close to her mouth but gave enough space to move freely and allow her to drink without restriction but to restrict her grass intake. Well, as I expected, she HATED it. I watched her initially as she was getting more and more frustrated, shaking her head and pawing at the grass. Then, she wouldn't try at all and would just keep coming back to me as if to say, 'For God's sake, take it off me you cruel woman.'

It broke my heart seeing her so fed up but laminitis is so serious I had no option. At this point, I was confident I'd caught it early enough before the pedal bone in her feet had had chance to rotate. If this had happened, then it would have probably have been game over. I had to walk away and leave her to work it out for herself. She's a clever mare so I had every confidence in her. After an hour, she hadn't attempted to eat and came down to stand on the yard so I took the muzzle off and put her back in the stable with the next soaked hay net. She was clearly hungry. I would try again tomorrow. I was not prepared to leave her out hungry for hours on end because this might cause colic and having been there in the most serious way possible years ago, I was not taking any chances.

Every day I turned her out for an hour and she soon got the hang of the muzzle, to my relief. Her routine eventually became grazing out at night and being stabled throughout the day. It didn't take long before she was shod and being ridden again.

I continued with the routine but bouts of laminitis occurred again followed by mild bouts of colic. These colic episodes were becoming a daily occurrence. She would stop part way through her feed or hay net and look at her flanks, then stretch herself and get down to roll. She looked totally fed up. But before I had a chance to call the vet, she would be OK again.

After a consultation with the vet, it was recommended Breeze would be scoped to check for ulcers. I had to starve her from 9pm the night before, which didn't go down too well. She loves routine and when breakfast didn't arrive and she was being loaded into a trailer instead, she was not happy about that either. Once we arrived at the vet's clinic, Breeze was taken off to be scoped. I had also requested her feet be X-rayed so we could see if the laminitis had caused any damage to her pedal bones.

The results were in, she had ulcers which were quite nasty and a couple were bleeding. Poor girl, no wonder she was uncomfortable. Still, they could be treated with regular weekly injections for the next month and prescribed medication which was to be added twice a day to her food. The injections were horrific. I've never seen such a large needle and amount of liquid in a syringe, injected straight into her rump. She hated it. However, the X-rays proved there was a very slight rotation of the pedal bones but nothing serious.

A month later we went back to the clinic for a further scope. The vet asked me for permission to run blood tests for Cushing's disease as she felt this might have been an under lying issue and she wanted to either rule it in or out.

More bad news followed; the ulcers had gone but she was diagnosed with Cushing's. Cushing's is a complex progressive disease of the pituitary gland and the treatment is medication for life. I was really surprised about this news as she had not shown any of the obvious signs? The medication comes in the form of a small tablet which has to be taken daily. Luckily Breeze is very food orientated, she takes the tablet from my hand mixed in with some balancer. Six weeks on, she hasn't had any more bouts of colic and continues on a strict routine for laminitis. She will be monitored with regular bloods tests from now on.

I appreciate Breeze is twenty-seven years old. I am still riding her and she still loves going out. I'm still waiting for her to stop spooking and slow down but I don't think this will ever happen! Tilly is twenty-eight years old and apart from showing slight signs of arthritis, is also still being ridden and still going strong.

I am very lucky to have found my two beautiful mares. I've had Breeze for seventeen years, Tilly for twelve years and they have certainly been a huge part of my life. They will both end their days here with me when they retire and I cherish every single day I have left with them.

It's been fifty-two years since my grandfather started me on this journey by taking me to a local riding stable and sitting me on a pony.

Who knows what the future holds for me? Maybe another horse or two? I'm sure my husband will have something to say about this so I'll have to wait and see!